HEROES, VILLAINS, AND HEALING:

A Guide to Help Male Survivors of Child Sexual Abuse

Using DC Comic Superheroes and Villains

Kenneth Rogers Jr.

Strategic Book Publishing and Rights Co.

Strategic Book Publishing and Rights Co., LLC
USA | Singapore
www.sbpra.com

For information about special discounts for bulk purchases, please contact Strategic Book Publishing and Rights Co., LLC. Special Sales, at bookorder@sbpra.net.

ISBN: 978-1-946539-38-0

Review Requested:

If you loved this book, would you please provide a review at Amazon.com?

Thank You

Thanks, Susan.

Table of Contents

Introduction

Let me begin with an apology and a warning. If you are reading this book to understand the nuances of DC superheroes, the place of their origins, and the time of their demise, I'm sorry, but this is not the book for you. Although I have read many comics and watched countless animated series, movies, and motion pictures, I am in no way, shape, or form an expert on the specifics of the DC universe. This book is for survivors of child sexual abuse, or partners of survivors of child sexual abuse, seeking to understand the nature of their trauma and how it has had negative and positive effects throughout their life. The use of superheroes is meant to help male survivors see and understand themselves, actions, emotions, and way of life in the archetypes of the heroes they love and villains they love to hate. This book is meant to start male survivors on the journey to understanding and healing from their sexual abuse.

Unfortunately, I am not an expert in trauma. I am simply a survivor who has researched, explored, and sought help for my sexual abuse through therapy, meditation, and medication. This means the information I provide in this book is incomplete. For true, lasting healing you must seek help through therapy and counseling. My reason for writing this book is because I wanted to help other male survivors of sexual abuse, allowing them to hear the story and perspective of childhood sexual trauma from another male survivor.

Much of the information and strength I gathered were from female survivors, notably in the book *The Courage to Heal* by Ellen Bass and Laura Davis. The coping strategies I gathered from my therapist, Susan Todd, LCSW-C. Although the information provided has been beyond beneficial, and I wouldn't be here today without them, in many cases I felt alone as the only male survivor to experience this abuse. I did not, and do not, want other male survivors to feel the same isolation. I want them to see their trauma as a source of strength in the characters they may identify with as superheroes. Use this book as a guide toward beginning to understand your childhood sexual abuse and beginning the process of healing.

Was I Sexually Abused?

As you begin to read these pages, you may ask yourself, "Was I sexually abused as a child?" There is no easy way to answer this question, because admitting the answer would mean acknowledging your weakness as a child, the abuse you survived, and the healing journey you are beginning.

Before beginning to reflect on your past to answer this difficult question, take a moment to acknowledge that you are not alone. There are other survivors. Other males have experienced sexual trauma in their childhood and grown stronger as adults after coming to terms with, and mourning the loss of, the childhood they were forced to endure. To know if you were sexually abused as a child or teen, some questions you may ask yourself are:

- Was I raped or otherwise penetrated?
- Was I forced to penetrate someone else?
- Was I made to watch sexual acts?
- Was I forced to perform oral sex?
- Was I made to pose naked for an adult's gratification?
- Was I made to fondle another male or female against my will?
- Was I forced to take part in ritualized abuse in which I was physically, psychologically, or sexually tortured?

I understand these are not easy questions to answer. However, if you answered yes to any of the questions, you have come a long way. I commend you for surviving and know the pain you endured was real and should not be minimized in any way. As you begin to reflect on your sexual abuse and your approach to healing, you may feel lost, confused, and unable to interpret your role in the sexual abuse. This is normal. Take time to process these thoughts. Throughout this book, you will be asked to participate in writing exercises, to journal, and to reflect on your past experiences. Knowing you were abused, who abused you, and being able to tell your story is one of the first steps toward understanding your trauma. This is difficult, but necessary, and may not be able to be done yet. Take your time. Stop reading if it is necessary. Rest, reflect, and return and when you are ready.

Part One:
Heroes

A hero is no braver than an ordinary man, but he is brave five minutes longer.

-Ralph Waldo Emerson

Chapter One
Am I A Hero?

It is safe to say our society has become inundated with superheroes. No longer is the world of red capes, magic rings, super speed, and unimaginable strength simply for prepubescent boys, geeks, nerds, and middle-aged adult men who failed to launch from their parent's basement. Instead, superheroes dominate the silver screen with Marvel's *Avengers* and DC's *Dawn of Justice*; television shows such as *Arrow, Flash, Gotham, Jessica Jones, Luke Cage,* and *Daredevil*; and throughout pop culture as reputable actors such as Benedict Cumberbatch, Robert Downey Jr., Will Smith, and Ben Affleck are placed as lead roles in blockbuster films such as *Dr. Strange, Iron Man, Suicide Squid,* and *Batman vs. Superman: Dawn of Justice*.

We have come to idolize these fictional characters, and as a survivor of child sexual abuse, many of the personality traits you adopted to survive can be seen in the actions and beliefs of these heroes. Although these personality traits may have served you well over the years, eventually these traits, actions, and emotions will turn against you. The only way to ensure permanent growth and healing toward remaining a survivor and not a victim is to understand these traits and how they are a result of the sexual abuse you experienced as a child. This part of the book examines the characteristics of different superheroes and how their secrets, superhuman abilities, adventures, and fears can help you understand the nature of your trauma.

Chapter Two
Flash: The Hero Code

Life is locomotion. If you're not moving, you're not living. But there comes a time when you've got to stop running away from things and you've got to start running towards something. You've got to forge ahead. Keep moving. Even if your path isn't lit, trust that you'll find your way.

—*The Flash (New 52) Vol. 1, No. 1*

The Boy Code

In the winter issue of DC's *All Star Comics #3*, the Justice Society of America (JSA) was born. Like Marvel's Avengers, and DC's Justice League, this was the first uniting of heroes who, at the time, lived in their own separate universes, oblivious of the others' existence. Each had their own separate adventures until they were united into one action-packed comic that readers could enjoy.

The first JSA heroes were the Flash, the Atom, Doctor Fate, Green Lantern, Hawkman, Sandman, and the Spectre. While the birth of the JSA is amazing as a lover of heroes and understanding where they originated, this is not what's of interest when understanding the hero code. Instead, what is of interest is a letter sent to boys and girls of the JSA fan club.

In 1942, as the first American forces arrived in Europe during World War II, and Anne Frank made the first entries in her diary as a thirteen-year-old girl, children across America were joining the Junior Justice Society of America (JJSA). When joining the JJSA, they received a letter bordered in American flags and speckled with the images of their favorite heroes of the JSA. In this letter, the JSA state the recipient is now an official member of the JJSA and "pledge to do everything possible to uphold the cause of justice; to obey The Golden Rule: 'Do unto others as you would have them do unto you.' Never be guilty of prejudice or discrimination against a fellow human being because of race, creed, or color!" The letter was signed by then JSA secretary, Wonder Woman, Deana Prince.

What's striking is that this letter hits at the heart of the superhero code. As a male survivor of child sexual abuse, the hero code is what defined my existence as a child. In the world of heroes and comics, whether on television or on the art filled pages, heroes were predictable. They followed a code. No matter if one hero vowed never to use a gun, could fly, or move at lightning speed, they all had a code never to kill and to protect and defend the weak. This predictability is what made them safe, and safety is what child sexual abuse survivors need more than anything else. This is because survivors of child sexual abuse, whether female or male, never feel safe. That safety was taken away when their bodies were forced to no longer belong to them. As a child, I needed this code to define my life, and it has. I have taken the vow and live under a code of my own I dare not break. The consequences would be too severe to bear and originate from my own psyche.

Teaching children to embody this code of justice and order over might did not begin with the JJSA. It came years before comics were a mainstream hit, and can be seen in the Boy Scouts of America handbook of 1911. On its pages, the Boy Scouts provided its young men with the history of chivalry and how it was the responsibility of its members to uphold the beliefs of truth and democracy in today's society. It states:

> So today there is a demand for a modern type of chivalry. It is for this reason that Boy Scouts of America have come into being. Chivalry began in the distant past out of the desire to help others, and the knights of the older days did this as best they could. Now the privilege and responsibility comes to the boys of today, and the voices of the knights of the olden times and the hardy pioneers of our own country are urging boys of today to do the right thing, in a gentlemanly way, for the sake of those about them. All of those men, whether knights or pioneers, had an unwritten code, somewhat like our scout law, and their motto was very much like the motto of the Boy Scouts, "Be prepared."

This unwritten code is why male survivors, like me, especially love heroes. In the world of comics there are no gray areas. There is only black or white, right or wrong, good or evil, hero or villain. It is difficult to admit, but in reality, there are no heroes and villains. There are only humans and healing. Neither heroes nor villains are individuals to aspire to become, but they can be guides for survivors to help understand their own strengths and areas of improvement.

Although the hero code has no definite truth, there are truths we must come to understand if the rape and incest culture in our society is ever going to change. Various statistics state one in three girls and one in six boys are sexually abused by the time they reach the age of eighteen. The Rape Abuse and Incest National Network (RAINN) states that 1 in 33 men will be sexually abused in their lifetime. However, male sexual abuse is a topic most people do not want to discuss. These people believe sexual abuse, mental abuse, and incest should and must remain locked away, but these topics must be talked about. Senseless acts of violence that cause physical and emotional scars that last a lifetime continue to happen behind closed and locked doors, eventually forcing the locks to be jimmied and the demons inside to come pouring out like the sins and evils of Pandora's box. Many of these thoughts and beliefs began as boys.

From a young age, boys are socialized into following the "boy code," described by William S. Pollack, associate clinical professor of psychology at Harvard Medical School, and author of *Real Boys: Rescuing Our Sons from the Myths of Boyhood*, as:

1. **The sturdy oak:** Men should be stoic, independent and refrain from showing weakness.

2. **Give 'em hell:** Boys and men should be macho, take risks, and use violence.

3. **The big wheel:** Men should demonstrate their power and dominance and how they've got everything under control, even when they don't.

4. **No sissy stuff:** Real men don't cry or display emotions that might be viewed as feminine; doing so leaves men open to being labeled as "sissies" or "fags."

The indoctrination of these stereotypes at such a young age leads men toward the path of suffering in silence and self-medication in the form of drugs and alcohol abuse. Society tells these young men to hold in their emotions, deal with them personally, and that given enough time they will go away. These beliefs lead to alcohol and other substance-related disorders, sleep disorders, pyromania, intermittent explosive disorder, pathological gambling, and sexual disorders such as exhibitionism, pedophilia, and voyeurism, according to the Prevention Institute in 2014.

To prevent the cycle of this behavior, men and boys need to know it is okay to share their feelings, seek help for overcoming their sexual abuse and mental disorders, and move toward healing. This, however, is difficult. The norms established by the boy code drive men toward feelings of stress, anxiety, inadequacy, and depression when they believe they are not living up to unfair expectations. This makes seeking help difficult, and generally makes mental health support groups unsuited for men.

For men and young boys to be open to discussing their abuse, they must first feel safe and able to relate to their counselor, therapist, or individuals in their support group. Because many counselors, therapists, and survivors in support groups are not men, they steer clear of seeking help. This means that healing must be done in creative ways that allow the safety needed to express themselves, their emotions, and their abuse. Healing circles within communities grounded in indigenous/cultural values are a key method to engage men and boys of color specifically when dealing with healing (Prevention Institute, 2014). This means getting men to open up must be done creatively and safely to allow exploration into their own abuse as survivors.

This is what *Heroes, Villains, and Healing Men of Child Sexual Abuse* does. It allows men and boys to view themselves and their actions through the eyes of the heroes and villains of the comics they love. To understand why this book is of importance, we must move away from the boy code and allow the opportunity for you to examine the hero code you may have developed for yourself as a survivor. Over the years, it has been this hero code of "right over might" that appeals to people the world over, and you as a male survivor of child sexual abuse.

Instead of locking the knowledge of your abuse behind closed doors, they must be opened. Healing must be allowed to take place. To do so means confronting and conquering each demon before moving to the next. This also means making abusers accountable for their actions. This is not easy. It takes time, but it is worth it if it means becoming the person you were meant to be and beginning the process of healing from your sexual abuse. To begin this process, we will examine the positives and negatives of the hero code you may have developed through the exploration of the superhero the Flash and the three heroes who have worn the costume of the Crimson Crusader over the years: Jay Garrick, Barry Allen, and Wally West.

The Hero Code

Superheroes have a code in which they live by. This code defines who they are as a hero. For some, like Batman, it means never using a gun. For others, like Superman, it means being a beacon of hope that never waivers. It's this code of right over might that appeals to people the world over and you as a male survivor of child sexual abuse. The absolutes of right and wrong of the comics may be the same way you see the world. You, like a superhero, have trained yourself to believe an idea of the way things *must* be no matter the circumstance. In some cases, it is a benefit. It informs your decisions about not being an offender, not to hurt yourself or others, and to not give up. However, it can also be a hindrance. It leads you to believe in absolute thinking about yourself and the world around you.

For example, this absolute thinking may lead you to believe that real men don't get help, real men don't cry, real men don't show their feelings, and real men can't be raped. This hero code can lead to some good, but it can also stifle growth, because reality is not simply black or white, right or wrong. Gray areas exist in our world from moment to moment in every day of our lives. Although each hero has threads of the same code throughout their being that separate their behavior from those of villains, Barry Allen's Flash is the most genuine and honest of all the heroes in the DC Universe. It's through Barry's life, death, and eventual resurrection that you can understand that without a little give and understanding of humanity the hero code/guide to becoming a survivor can become a villain's motto.

Sacrifice and Overcoming Limitations

In 1985's *Crisis on Infinite Earths #8,* "A Flash of Lightning," Barry dies as the Flash while saving the universe from complete annihilation when an anti-matter cannon threatens to destroy all of existence (dramatic, I know, but it's a comic). To prevent this from happening, Barry runs at super speed around the cannon to contain its blast and cause it to implode on itself. As Barry begins, and with each step afterward, the cannon consumes more and more of his ability to run. However, with each passing moment he pushes himself to run faster than he has ever run in the past, causing him to be sucked from reality into the stream of time. Each frame of Barry's movement around the cannon depicts the gruesome image of Barry wasting away into nothing, until all that is left of the hero is his ring and uniform. The story ends with a quote from poet William Knox: "Oh, why should the spirit of mortal be proud? Like a fast-flittering meter, a fast-flying cloud, a flash of the lightning, a break of the wave, he passes from life to his rest in the grave."

Barry's sacrifice of his own life to save the entire universe may define a large part of the hero code you have created for yourself as a survivor of child sexual abuse and the belief that sacrifice for the well-being of others is far greater than the well-being of yourself, even if it means sacrificing yourself in the process. The evidence of Barry's self-sacrifice can be seen in his final words of the comic before his death. He states, "There's hope, there's always hope. Time to save the world!" What he says is not very long, but it portrays the optimism of his character and his desire to help others.

Although enforcing his idea of what it means to be a hero led to Barry's eventual death, he saved countless lives. Barry's interpretation of the hero code guided his actions toward sacrifice, caring, and compassion in the same way you, as a male survivor of child sexual abuse, continue to strive toward living, breathing, and providing for the people around you in every way you can, even if it means your own self-sacrifice. (The topic of self-sacrifice will be explored more in the next chapter.) It also reinforces the belief that you can always do more, push yourself harder, and overcome any obstacle placed before you if you work and try hard enough. This is evident in Barry's push to run faster than he had ever run before, even with greater restrictions on his speed because of the power of the anti-matter cannon.

Being a survivor may mean, to you, having the same understanding and empathy as Barry in "A Flash of Lightning." Although this form of absolute thinking in the hero code has the ability for good, it can also have the effect of limiting thinking and stifling growth. It can steer you as a male survivor of child sexual abuse toward seeking absolute perfection, rather than acknowledging your effort. It has the potential to limit your vision and place blinders on the way you view your actions so that you only see your failures. These limitations of the hero code make it impossible to live up to the code of heroism and sacrifice you have possibly created and placed on yourself as a male survivor. This means finding it difficult to acknowledge your possible flaws, shortcomings, and humanity, which is key to healing from the trauma of child sexual abuse. In short, it prevents happiness. These hindrances of the hero code, and the possible negative effects of your absolute thinking as a male survivor, can best be understood through the third incarnation of the Flash, Wally West, the nephew of Iris West, Barry Allen's wife.

Finding Your Identity and Living for You

When Barry dies in the "Flash of Lightning," he is replaced as the Flash by Wally West. Wally had already been a "Speedster" (this is the name given to people who have the ability to run at superfast speeds and can tap into the "Speed Force") and superhero for a number of years as Kid Flash when he acquired his abilities in the same way as Barry, but at a much younger age. However, when Barry died, he put away Kid Flash and became the Flash permanently. However, when this occurred, Wally lost a large portion of the speed he once possessed as Kid Flash.

For many years, he never understood why he was a fraction of the hero he used to be, so he decided to seek answers by visiting a therapist in the 1998's "The Unforgiving Minute" in *Secret Origins Annual #2*. It's in this issue readers learn of Barry's unwavering hero code when he was alive, and how adopting the hero code of another person, rather than creating and developing your own, even if it's someone you look up to and respect, can be devastating to your mental health.

The story begins with Wally sitting in the office of a therapist decorated with a small lounge couch, desk, coffee maker, books, and a skyline of a major metropolitan city. Wally proceeds to tell the therapist he is there to try and get his speed back to where it was when he was a kid. He also tells the therapist about Barry and how his speed used to be the same as the now dead Speedster. He says:

> Barry was so fast he could race the beam of a flashlight or enter other dimensions. He could do anything. For a little while, I knew what it was like to have that speed, and I want it back. I can't seem to hold onto anything. Barry's dead. My dad's gone. I had six million dollars and I blew it away. You know Barry never had any money. Just a cop's salary. But he sure was happier with it than I was with all my money.

He explains how he got his powers after being hit with a lightning bolt and doused with chemicals the same way as Barry, his crime fighting career as Kid Flash, and his work as a member of the Teen Titans. Afterward, he tells the doctor, "See, I know what you think of me, Doc. You think I'm spoiled, selfish, and weak . . . that all I'm interested in are chicks and fame . . . that if people knew about me they'd think I was a real jerk . . . that I deserved to lose my money for acting stupid."

The therapist asks Wally what he thinks Barry would think if he were still alive. Wally says that Barry would be hurt and disappointed that he turned out that way, but the therapist doesn't buy it. Instead, he explains how Wally is making Barry harder on him in death than he would ever be if he were alive. Next, he tells Wally to write the number of people he's saved in the past ten years. Wally writes the number 172, and the therapist is shocked at such a high number. He explains to Wally how he saved each of those people's lives, and that every one of those people was important, so he should not beat himself up, because he made a difference in their lives. Finally, he tells Wally he has imposter's syndrome. This is a mental disorder that boys feel when they lose impressive father figures. The therapist tells Wally that, because he held Barry on such a high pedestal as a hero, he feels that nothing he earns is truly his and that he's afraid of being revealed as a fraud. He says that Barry is holding Wally back and that the only way to reach his full potential was to ease up and allow himself to be happy and alive, even if Barry was dead. When the hour of therapy comes to an end, Wally is left alone to think of the past, his powers, the lives he saved, and the mentor he lost.

As a male survivor of child sexual abuse, you may view yourself and your actions in the same way as Wally. You attempt to predict what people are thinking of you and your actions, in an attempt to live up to impossibly perfect expectations you may put on yourself. This is called "mind reading." This means you judge your actions through the eyes of others rather than your own accomplishments. Your impostor's syndrome may stem from fictional superheroes, fathers, father figures, or stereotypical beliefs of how a male should act or think.

In the same way Wally is held back by the beliefs of who he should be, rather than who he is and what he should do, you may be held back from true healing of the sexual trauma you suffered as a child. This kind of absolute thinking of the hero code leads to absolutes that can only be bent and eventually broken. While the hero code is an excellent guide for survivors to live through the trauma of their sexual abuse as children, it can become detrimental as an adult. Without accepting your humanity, weakness, and trauma you suffered as a child, you risk unknowingly breaking the hero code you developed, possibly becoming an offender; rather than being the hero, you become the villain. While it may seem impossible, the roles of hero and villain can become reversed in the same way Barry Allen became his own worst enemy in Geoff Johns' graphic novel, *Flashpoint.*

Hero to Villain

In the five-part epic graphic novel *Flashpoint,* Barry Allen lives as the Flash after being resurrected from the Speed Force during his death in *Crisis on Infinite Earths* (long story short, it's a comic book; go with it). When Barry returns to reality, he decides to save the life of the one person he couldn't when he was a boy and did not have his powers: his mother. To save her, Barry uses his super speed to travel into the past to stop his mother from being murdered. He succeeds at saving his mother, but when he returns to the present, reality has been altered. He soon realizes he is no longer the Flash, people who were once heroes have become villains, villains have become heroes, and Bruce Wayne never becomes Batman; instead, it is Bruce's father, Thomas Wayne. Seeing the changes, Barry immediately blames his archnemesis, Eobard Thawne, for altering the time stream and changing reality. Throughout the graphic novel, it never occurs to Barry that his actions are what caused such massive changes to the reality he knew. He thought saving one person's life and changing the past in such a small way could not have such a drastic effect.

The novel comes to an end when Thawne reveals to Barry that he was individual responsible for creating this alternate reality when he made the selfish decision to alter the past and save his mother. Knowing this, Barry makes the difficult decision to let his mother's murder occur the way it did in the past, saving the world (again), and restoring the reality he knew to exist.

Reading *Flashpoint* and understanding the reasons that motivated Barry's actions are key to understanding how the hero code you have created for yourself has the potential to lead to your downfall. Before the moment Barry makes the decision to alter his actions, he transforms from the hero to the villain. This is because he was blaming someone else for the problems he created. Throughout *Flashpoint*, Geoff Johns transforms Barry from a survivor to a victim. Johns transforms the hero code, meant to be flexible guidelines to help differentiate positive actions from those that are negative, into absolute thinking and uncompromising beliefs. When this occurred, Barry was no longer a hero, in the same way survivors can become victims. Both survivors and victims have suffered trauma against their will at the hands of someone else, in the same way heroes and villains acquire their powers. However, how the two view themselves and the world makes all the difference. Survivors know they were victimized and have suffered trauma, but they take responsibility for their actions after they were victimized. Survivors do not blame their trauma for all the mishaps in their life.

Victims blame the trauma they suffered as the source of all their problems socially, emotionally, and physically. This is how and why Barry became a victim/villain in *Flashpoint* and what you may be in danger of becoming if you do not seek help and healing.

It is important to understand that viewing yourself and your actions as those of a hero or villain is not the goal of this book. It is true that some social, mental, and physical problems in your life can be traced as a direct cause of the sexual abuse you suffered as a child. It's also true that ignoring the trauma you suffered as a child can only lead to further disasters, as it did in Barry's life. However, what you must understand is that heroes and villains are both wrong but should lead to healing. Knowing, understanding, and accepting the trauma you suffered as a child, working toward overcoming their effects, and living a life you control and take responsibility for is the only way to move beyond codes toward living and truly becoming the person you were meant to be.

Chapter Three
Superman: The Façade

Dreams save us. Dreams lift us up and transform us. And on my soul, I swear until my dream of a world where dignity, honor and justice becomes the reality we all share I'll never stop fighting. Ever.

—Superman, *Action Comics #175 (2001)*

Action Comics #1

In June of 1938, Superman was born on the cover of *Action Comics #1*. Jerry Siegel and Joe Shuster co-created a hero that would survive decades into the future, moving from the colorful pages of comics, to voices on the radio, comic strips in local newspapers, animated and live action television series, before becoming larger than life on the silver screen. Although it was the first official appearance of the Kryptonian hero, it's interesting to note how Superman does not take on the persona of a hero on the cover, but could easily be misinterpreted as a villain through the eyes of a young child.

Before projecting previous knowledge of Superman's heroic deeds and reaching the conclusion that the red-caped crusader is smashing the car as an act of heroism to stop some no-good thugs from committing a crime, the cover art can be viewed through the lens of a boy in the 1930s who has just seen Superman for the first time. The reason for this is because, in the 1930s, superheroes did not exist. Up until Superman's appearance in 1938, comic books were simple comics. They were funny, humorous, and designed to get a laugh from their readers with goofy characters placed in hilarious situations. Those were the books that sold, so those were the stories that were drawn and published. This means the modern comic books of today did not exist. So, a boy picking up *Action Comics #1* for the first time in 1938, seeing a man lifting a Chevy above his head and smashing it to pieces, had no idea what to think.

On the cover, the image is an array of colors, but none indicating righteousness or purity. In the background, yellow explodes forward, bringing to life the gleaming, green Chevy. This yellow background could be viewed as a representative motif of honesty and righteousness, if it wasn't contrasted by the car's broken fender and crippled hood as it is being smashed against a large boulder.

What also leaves the reader wary of who is the hero and who is the villain in this situation are the expressions and actions on each character of the cover. Two men dressed in suits are seen running out of the frame of the picture. The man fleeing toward the reader holds his head and wears an expression of sheer horror as he runs for his life. The final gentleman, on his hands and knees near the demolished car, seems shocked beyond belief. Unable to make sense of the situation, he lies there, waiting for it to end.

Finally, there's Superman. Comic book readers of 1938 had no idea *who* Superman was, let alone *what* he was. Superheroes did not exist, so they had no idea what a superhero was or what they represented. This means the red cape, blue tights, and gold plated chest with a red *S* meant nothing. Instead, all that was seen through the eyes of the reader when he viewed the cover of *Action Comics #1* is the impossible. He sees a man lifting a car and smashing it to pieces, as other men run for safety or cower in fear. Even the expression on the red-caped Superman reveals nothing of his intentions. He appears to find no joy in what he is doing, but he knows it has to be done.

Why am I mentioning this? It's because, in many ways, the boy from the 1930s holding *Action Comics #1* is a lot like you before your sexual abuse as a child. Before your sexual abuse, the only knowledge you had of good and evil were the innate senses you were born with. This lack of knowledge of sexual abuse and the ability to recognize a predator is what made you weak and vulnerable as a child. The abuser preys on innocence and transforms what was meant for good into something evil, without your knowing until it is too late. Like the young boy in 1938 holding *Action Comics #1*, and you as a male survivor of child sexual abuse, other survivors also are left alone to interpret themselves, their sexual abuse, and their abusers as being either a hero or a villain. Once sexual abuse occurs as a child, it shapes your view of the world and your interpretations of heroes, villains, survivors, and victims. After your abuse, in order to survive, your world becomes simple shades of black and white, with the absolutes of right and wrong and good and evil with no gray area between. Without help and healing, it shapes every aspect of your life as a survivor long after the comics and cartoons are stored away.

While reflecting and attempting to make sense of your abuse, you may not only feel like a young boy unable to make sense of the heroes and villains in your own world, but you may also feel powerless and weak.

Superman and the Façades Presented by Male Survivors of Child Sexual Abuse

Survivors of child sexual abuse feel isolated, because the positive self-esteem they were meant to develop as children was stripped away when their bodies were violated. According to *The Courage to Heal* (1992), this means you, as a survivor, may feel:

- bad, dirty, or ashamed;
- powerless, like a victim;
- different from other people;
- that there's something wrong deep down inside;

- that if people really knew you they'd leave.

This may also mean that as a male survivor you:

- hate yourself
- feel immobilized or can't get motivated
- are unable to protect yourself in dangerous situations
- have experienced repeated victimization as an adult
- struggle with self-destructive feelings or feel suicidal

As a male survivor of sexual abuse, you may have a hard time:

- identifying your own needs;
- nurturing and taking care of yourself;
- feeling good;
- trusting your intuition;
- recognizing your own interests, talents, or goals.

Some male survivors:

- are afraid to succeed
- can't accomplish the things they set out to do
- feel that they can never move forward in their lives
- feel compelled to be perfect
- forget whole chunks of their childhood

As a male survivor of child sexual abuse, you may never let others see your full range of emotions. This means creating a **façade or false identity** to cover your true feelings and appear socially acceptable to the people around you. On the surface you smile, work, and play, but beneath the surface, the trauma from the sexual abuse you suffered as a child cause you to rarely, if ever, let friends, family, or loved ones see the pain, suffering, and confusion brewing beneath.

This need to present a façade to the world in order to protect yourself, friends, family, and loved ones can best be seen in the same ways Superman presents a façade to the world to protect the people he cares for from discovering his true feelings and identity.

Superman attempts to live a normal life behind the alter ego of mild-mannered Clark Kent. You, as a survivor of child sexual abuse, may attempt to look and act normal to the rest of the world. However, beneath the surface there is a completely different person you have let few, if any, see.

These qualities make Superman an ideal character to help you understand how the effects of your sexual trauma have enforced a wall you have built to protect yourself and survive through the image of a façade. As a superhero, Superman's façades embody many of the traits of survivors in the form of lowered self-esteem and self-sacrifice for the greater good.

For example, Superman carries the weight of the world on his shoulders, believing he can do anything and feeling like a lesser hero when he does not succeed. You, as a survivor of child sexual abuse, may also feel like a lesser person unworthy of praise when you cannot accomplish a task with zero mistakes. This anxiety damages your self-esteem and makes you feel unworthy of love.

In many ways, you, as a survivor of sexual abuse, are similar to Superman and the different façades he presents to the world. You carry the weight of the world on your shoulders. You may often try to do and be perfect at every task you attempt. However, when you have no way of accomplishing each task with absolute perfection, you sacrifice your own health and well-being for the greater good. As a superhero, Superman often does the same. This idea of self-sacrifice and its effects on self-esteem can best be seen in the July 1958 issue of *Action Comics #242* and the glassed Kryptonian city of Kandor.

The City of Kandor

There are limits to Superman's abilities. It's a fact that sometimes makes it difficult for him to accept, just as it may be difficult for you to accept your own limitations as a survivor of sexual abuse. The effects of these limitations can have detrimental impacts on your self-esteem, in the same way as Superman. The limits of Superman's abilities and the effects of his self-esteem can be best seen and applied to your own self-esteem in *Action Comics #242*, "The Super-Duel in Space." It is in this comic that readers are first introduced to the city of Kandor and the villain Brainiac. Brainiac's scientific knowledge makes him an unbeatable opponent for the Man of Steel.

The story begins with Clark Kent, Lois Lane, and other reporters and astronauts launching into space on the experimental rocket, *Columbus*. As they are in orbit around Earth, the rocket encounters a flying saucer shooting electrified power beams at the *Columbus*. While inside the rocket, Clark uses his super-hearing as Superman to find out that the alien inside the flying saucer calls himself "Brainiac, master of super-scientific forces." Rather than stay and protect the people on board the *Columbus*, Clark quickly puts on a spacesuit and the only jet pack, opens the emergency escape hatch, and pretends to flee back to Earth. Lois sees Clark attempt to escape danger and says, "Poor Clark. He's so afraid, he's jumping back to Earth!" perpetuating the weak façade of Clark Kent before transforming into the strong alter ego of Superman.

When Superman approaches the *Columbus* and Brainiac's flying saucer, he attempts to attack the alien spacecraft, but is rebounded by an "ultra-force barrier." Instead, Superman uses his super strength to push the Columbus out of harm's way.

Rather than continue his journey through space, Brainiac begins filling large glass bottles with oxygen, shrinking major cities across Earth, and placing them inside the bottles to preserve the cities and the inhabitants. The artwork reveals London, Paris, Rome, and New York as being the four major cities Brainiac has captured. As the story continues, Brainiac explains how he plans to use the people in the bottles to repopulate his home world ravaged by a plague that killed all its denizens except himself. The location of Brainiac's planet and the name of his people is never said. However, in future issues of *Superman* and *Action Comics*, Brainiac's origin is rewritten to make him a major villain of Superman's, as the surviving computer system of Krypton that helped bring about its destruction.

Later, *Action Comics #242* cuts to Superman carrying about the *Columbus*. When he ensures the American rocket is safe, Superman returns to Brainiac's flying saucer and bottles the alien on a deserted planet in space while Brainiac recharges the hyper-batteries of his ship. During their battle, Superman's powers are of no help. Superman's heat vision is reflected back to the hero by the alien's power belt, which creates an "ultra-shell" of protection. As the battle continues, Superman proceeds to throw stalagmites, giant chunks of the planet, and larger pieces of space debris, before finally fleeing with an expression of pure horror.

The battle ends with Brainiac asking Superman, "Well? Want to continue the duel Puny Man?"

Superman replies, "No . . . No! I . . . I've had enough! I quit . . . I'm licked!"

While it appears to the reader and Brainiac that Superman has given up, he returns to Earth with a plan. The superhero lands in Metropolis just as the city is shrunk by Brainiac and placed in a glass bottle. Using his super strength and ability to fly, Superman escapes the bottle before it can be sealed. However, before he can use his abilities to return all the cities in bottles back to Earth in their original states, he is spotted by Brainiac and is believed to be a fly because he is so small. As Brainiac and his pet monkey, KoKo (weird, I know, but it's the 50s and I've learned to just go with it), attempt to swat the fly-sized superhero, Superman attempts to hide in a different uncorked bottle. Immediately, as he enters the bottle, Superman recognizes the city as being Kryptonian, as he begins to lose his powers and fall toward the surface of the planet.

Upon arrival, Superman meets Professor Kimda, the leading scientist of the city who happened to be Jor-El's (Kal-El's father) roommate in college (really?). As the two talk, Kimda explains to Superman how Brainiac stole Kandor, Krypton's capital, before the planet blew apart, and how Brainiac operates his hyper-force ray that allows him to shrink and enlarge entire cities. Because Superman has no powers in the Kryptonian city of Kandor, he is trapped with the rest of the Kryptonians.

Unable to come up with a plan of escape, Kimda shows Superman the wonders of their city. He shows him the rockets they manufacture in their factories, the exotic animals they keep in the Kryptonian zoo, the robots that farm their crops, and the artificial sun the Kandorians created to help light their perpetually dark bottle. Although the wonder of the Kryptonian people is presented to Superman, and the possibility of escape appears impossible, the Man of Steel refuses to revert to his Kryptonian alter ego of Kal-El. Instead, he continues to believe he can stop Brainiac from carrying out his evil plan, save the people of Kandor, replace the miniaturized cities back on Earth, and keep all three of his façades separate, secret, and intact.

Outside the bottle, Brainiac and KoKo enter suspended animation for the long journey to his world. Inside the bottle, Kimda and Superman make plans to escape using a rocket manufactured in the glassed city to pierce the lid of the bottle, and an exotic animal from the Kryptonian zoo that eats metal to chew a hole through the lid, creating a hole large enough for Superman to escape through and regain his powers.

When he escapes from Kandor, Superman uses his newly restored powers to activate Brainiac's hyper-force machine and enlarge and return all the cities to their correct locations on Earth. When all the cities from Earth have been restored, Superman plans to enlarge Kandor and place it on Earth for the citizens to have full lives. However, there is a problem. There is not enough power to enlarge the Kryptonian city *and* himself. In this situation, rather than Superman acknowledging his own weakness and inability to accomplish everything with perfection, he decides to sacrifice himself and enlarge Kandor instead. He thinks to himself:

> *"Only one charge of hyper-forces left, enough to restore the Krypton city to normal size or me, but not both! Well, I'm only one man! The hyper-ray can give a million people in the Krypton city, allowing them to live on Earth! I'll press the button that will liberate them!"*

However, before he can push the button to enlarge Kandor, a rocket shoots through the air and enlarges Superman instead. From the rocket emerges Kimda. He tells Superman he could not deprive Earth of its great superhero. Sad and still alone, Superman takes the bottle with the miniature Kandor from Brainiac's flying saucer as it continues in space and places it in his Fortress of Solitude in the North Pole, hoping to one day return the city to normal size and live with his people.

Rather than admit the limits of his abilities and his inability to save everyone, Superman decided to sacrifice himself. You, as a male survivor of child sexual abuse, may often feel the same way. Male survivors sometimes take the world on their shoulders. You may agree to take on more responsibilities than you can handle. When an obstacle gets in the way of your ability to simply power through, such as time, sleep, or happiness, your self-esteem cannot handle the thought of failure. You may beat yourself up by calling yourself names and treating your body as if it were your worst enemy. When this self-abuse is not enough to appease your already battered self-esteem, you may contemplate sacrificing yourself through suicide.

You may think to yourself, "If I can't do it all, what's the point in living, if I'm only going to be failure." These thoughts eat away at your psyche. You either get help, attempt suicide and fail, or attempt suicide and are stopped by a friend in the same way Kimda save Superman. This is why, according to the National Vital Statistics report of 2004 and the Center for Disease Control in 2009, that, compared to women, men are four to eighteen times more likely to kill themselves. Men are also four times more likely to die of suicide than women.

Young people are also at a higher risk of suicide. In 2011, the Center for Disease Control reported that almost 16 percent of students in grades nine to twelve have reported seriously considering suicide, and 7.8 percent reported attempting suicide in the past twelve months. It's for this reason that suicide is one of the top three causes of death among young people ages 15-24. These statistics reveal that men, and male survivors of sexual abuse, have low feelings of self-esteem when they feel they are not living up to expectations of what it means to be a "true man," and the only way to escape is through suicide. However, as a survivor of child sexual abuse, you must treat your body and mind with sympathy, acknowledging your shortcomings, knowing your weakness, and agreeing that you are not Superman. You are only human. Doing what you *can* when you can is the only way to remain a survivor and not become a victim. It's the only way to heal your self-esteem and begin to heal from your trauma.

Capacity for Intimacy

As a male survivor of child sexual abuse, you may rarely, if ever, let the people you care for see beyond the façade of strength and control you present to the world. The reason for this may be because of your belief that revealing your true emotions of fear, anxiety, and depression will cause others to view you negatively and take away the power you have gained over your life, making you weak. You may believe dropping your façade will leave you vulnerable, and to have a relationship in which people around you knew of your trauma would result in the destruction of your entire identity. These beliefs limit your capacity to be truly intimate with loved ones, because they never see who you truly at your best *and* worse. According to *The Courage to Heal* (1992), as a male survivor of child sexual abuse, you may find it difficult:

- to trust people
- to make close friends
- to create or maintain healthy relationships
- to give or receive nurturing
- to be affectionate
- to say no or set appropriate boundaries

As a male survivor, you may also:

- feel that you don't deserve love

- be afraid of people
- feel alienated or isolated
- rarely feel connected to yourself or others
- get involved with people who are inappropriate or unavailable
- don't know whom to trust or trust to readily
- frequently feel betrayed or taken advantage of
- have good friends but struggle in romantic or sexual relationships

Some male survivors:

- are unable to form lasting relationships;
- have trouble making commitments;
- shut down, get nervous, or panic when people get too close;
- cling to the people you care about;
- repeatedly test people to the point of sabotaging relationships;
- expect people to leave you;
- get involved with people who abuse you.

The belief that allowing people to understand your trauma would mean destroying a part of your identity, leaving you as a fragment of your former self, is not true. In fact, it is the exact opposite. Seeking help and leaning on loved ones for support fuses the façades you have created into a complete individual capable of all emotions, not just a select few. It is this black-and-white thinking that has resulted in isolation and loneliness that will continue until you make the decision to face your trauma and seek help to begin healing.

This lack of intimacy can also be seen Superman's façade. Superman is afraid to let himself be with anyone fully. He fears his own powers and isolates himself from others in the Fortress of Solitude. You, as a survivor of child sexual abuse, may keep friends, family, and loved ones at a distance. Like Superman, this is because of the fear of becoming weak and vulnerable, and reliving a time when you were powerless to stop your abuse.

The Girl in Superman's Past

This isolation and perpetuated belief that being intimate means relinquishing your strength can best be seen in *Superman #129*. It begins with Lois and Clark sitting in the cold watching a football game. As they watch, Clark notices a checkered blanket across Lois's legs, and he proceeds to have a flashback about a girl from his past, Lori Lemaris.

The flashback begins one afternoon when Clark Kent was in college. While on campus, he notices a girl in a wheelchair careening down a hill, out of control. To stop her in time, Clark uses his heat vision to melt the tires of the wheelchair and slow down the chair enough for him to run and help the girl at normal speed. Unfortunately, the melting of the tires causes the chair to stop suddenly and throw the girl forward into Clark's arms. Immediately, when their eyes meet, Clark becomes smitten with her blue eyes and her courage to continue her education even though she was paralyzed.

With the girl in his arms and the tires of the wheelchair melted, Clark attempts to come up with a valid excuse about the current situation. Before he can come up with one, the girl comes up with one for him. She says, "The speed of the wheels must have created so much friction heat that the rubber melted! That could explain it, couldn't it?"

Hearing the explanation, which he knew was not true, Clark thinks to himself, *She said that almost as if . . . as if we both knew it isn't true!*

Later, as the day continues, Clark continues to think of Lori, when, by accident, the college aquarium floods and he transforms into Superman. While wrangling the fish, he sees Lori in the tentacles of a giant octopus. Before Superman can save her, the octopus lets her go and flees, after seeing her lips move.

As Superman lifts her from the water, she makes up another excuse about why the octopus fled. "Well, Superman, he probably saw you streaking near and was frightened away."

Days pass and Clark spends more and more time with her, while having daydreams about flying Lori to see the planets, sculpting her image on Mount Everest, and flying an orchestra around the world so everyone could hear the love song he wrote for her. However, each night she has to be home by eight o'clock. Finally, Lori tells Clark they are having their last date, because she is returning home later that night.

As Lori rolls away, Clark realizes how much he loves her, can't live without her, and wants to marry her. He thinks to himself, *But my crime-fighting career as Superman would endanger my future wife! If criminals ever learned my Clark Kent identity, they could seize my wife as a hostage to force me to stop fighting them! There's only one way I can marry Lori and be sure she'll never be endangered! I must tell her my secret identity . . . then give up my Superman career and remain only in my Clark Kent identity!*

Later, Clark proposes to Lori at a romantic spot by the ocean. He attempts to tell her that he's Superman, but she stops him and says she already knows. Clark is shocked and wants to know how, but all she says is that it doesn't matter, she can't marry him, and that she has to be home by eight o'clock.

Clark is shocked, disappointed, and filled with questions. He follows Lori back to the trailer where she lives and uses his x-ray vision and super hearing to catch her making secret radio transmissions. Immediately, Clark considers her to be a spy. He searches her room when she leaves and discovers no bed, just a tank of salt water. When he sees this, he understands. He finds Lori, but before he can say a word, his telescopic vision reveals the bursting of a dam. He attempts to leave to stop the flood, but Lori says she can help.

Superman flies her to the scene of the flood, and she jumps from her wheelchair to reveal that she's a mermaid (That's right, a mermaid. It's best to suspend disbelief for a moment and remember this was also written for kids in the 50s) Both Superman and Lori work together to save homes, people, and subside the flood.

Afterward, Lori reveals how she is a denizen of the lost city of Atlantis. She explains how her people mastered the ability to read minds (thus how she discovered Clark's secret identity as Superman) and converted their race into mermen and mermaids. Lori also reveals how every one hundred years her people sends someone to the surface to learn of about progress on the surface. Lori was chosen for the task these hundred years, and now she has to return to Atlantis. After the explanation, Superman understands why they cannot be together and that he has to let her go, but not before a passionate underwater kiss as the comic comes to an end.

In *Superman #129:* "The Girl in Superman's Past," Clark felt as though the only way to be truly intimate with the woman he loved was to sacrifice one of his identities. He felt as though the only way he could love her, protect her, and have her love him in return was to be who she wanted him to be and would provide the most protection. As a male survivor, you may have the same feelings as Clark about revealing the nature of your abuse and trauma to the people who you love.

If you are in a relationship, you may have the urge to tell your partner about the trauma you suffered as a child, and you should. However, you should not believe revealing the nature of your abuse will rid you of the façade you carry as a survivor. That takes time and therapy. However, telling the people closest to you about the trauma you suffered strengthens the survivor identity you carry and moves you closer toward integrating your façades into one complete identity. Rather than attempting to live behind the façades of Superman and mild-mannered Clark Kent (which may have helped you survive your trauma as a child), begin the process of healing by recognizing these façades and becoming a complete individual. This process takes time, patience, therapy, and work you have already begun by reading this book.

When you make the decision to be fully intimate with the people closest to you and tell them of your sexual abuse, you may expect a specific reaction that matches the scene you have played in your head, in the same way Clark expected Lori to respond to the realization that he was Superman with shock and amazement. Instead, the conversation went completely different than expected for the Man of Steel. Rather than shock and amazement, Lori was calm, level-headed, and said she already knew. When this happened, Clark was beside himself with amazement and a little resentment.

When you decide to reveal your sexual abuse and drop the façade you have carried, the reactions of your loved ones may not be what you expect. You must brace yourself for that situation. You may expect them to react one way, such as with sympathy and compassion, but instead they react differently, such as with anger, contempt, and scorn. Being fully intimate and integrating the façade of the survivor into the personality you reveal to the world at all times means working toward the process where you reveal your sexual abuse without expecting a certain reaction. You reveal your abuse as a fact, not needing sympathy, kindness, or words of compassion, but as a truth. This takes time, practice, and the help of a therapist.

As a male survivor of child sexual abuse, you may feel alone and isolated from the rest of the world. You may feel as though you are not deserving of love because of your perceived weakness, but you deserve to be a complete person capable of all your emotions, love, and intimacy. Limiting who you truly are is not fair to you or the people close to you. You can be more than simply Superman. You can be you, which is much stronger than any Man of Steel, whether you fully believe it or not. You're stronger than you believe. This book may be only the beginning of your journey toward becoming a survivor and no longer a victim. You must do the work to seek the help you deserve and become the person you were meant to be.

Chapter Four
Batman: The Workaholic

A hero can be anyone. Even a man doing something as simple and reassuring as putting a coat around a little boy's shoulder to let him know that the world hadn't ended.

—Batman, *The Dark Knight Rises*

Detective Comics #33

The origins of Batman in the 1939 *Detective Comics #33* are beautifully written and drawn by Bill Finger and Bob Kane. In each panel, the use of green, reddish orange, yellow, and black allow each panel to explode from the page and scream to be read and inspected.

In the first panel, Bruce Wayne sees his parents die after being shot by a thug on the streets of Gotham City. Unlike modern comics or television, there is no blood. There is only the reddish orange of his mother's blouse as both parents lay motionless on the cement. The next panel is the last hint of innocence Bruce has before beginning his transformation into the Dark Knight. Behind Bruce, Kane uses green and yellow to signify innocence, honesty, and childhood, as it provides the backdrop of Bruce's shock and tears as he comes to the realization his parents are, "Dead! They're D-dead." From that moment on, the image of seeing his dead parents haunts every facet of his reality.

Bruce kneels and takes an oath. He says, "And I swear by the spirits of my parents to avenge their deaths by spending the rest of my life warring on all criminals." The montage moves forward to show Bruce learning chemistry, growing strong, and declaring he was now ready to begin his war on crime. What's most interesting is how the death of his parents (specifically, the sight of his mother) haunts every aspect of his innocence. Each panel contains the same reddish orange of his mother's blouse. It emanates from the bedside candle where he takes the oath, it surrounds him as he studies to prepare for the unpredictable, it radiates from his body while lifting a dumbbell over his head, and becomes a part of every part of the life he has built as it becomes engrained in the walls, furniture, and curtains of Wayne Manor, before becoming a part of the city he has entered as the Batman in the rooftops and buildings.

Bruce Wayne's abuse affected every nuance of his existence, in many ways without him knowing. It's true he made the oath to avenge their death and spent his entire life to prepare, but he had no idea it had become his life. He didn't, and couldn't have known the trauma had become the house in which he lived, the objects in his day-to-day life, or the way in which he saw every piece of the world. Every aspect of his life, every relationship, fact learned, muscle produced, and scar earned would be infected with the trauma of losing his childhood—which can also be said to be true for the effects of child sexual abuse.

Every piece of existence in the life of an adult who has been sexually abused as a child is tainted without their knowing. Like Bruce Wayne, victims of child sexual abuse build their foundation on the one moment their innocence was lost. The abuse becomes the walls and furniture of their home; the eyes, words, moments, and expressions of their children, spouses, and friends; their careers; the cars they drive; and the situations they avoid due to fear and anxiety.

What you, as a survivor of sexual abuse, must realize is that Batman is fiction. Unlike most victims, Bruce Wayne knows he is afraid. Every moment of every day he is deathly afraid of the life he's built, the precautions he's made, and the walls he's built will come crashing down. This is because children who have been sexually abused feel powerless, as if they have no sense of control. This means they must find some way to take back the control that was taken from them. Bruce Wayne prepares for every possible situation, to make sure he is prepared when and if something goes wrong. Victims of child sexual abuse often feel isolated and alone, as if there is no one they can truly trust. These are all the qualities of Bruce Wayne.

However, what make Batman an impossible fictional character is that he surrounds himself in his fears. He embodies them in the form of a bat, not to fight the fear he has of his reality, but instead to immerse himself in the isolation, paranoia, and distrust. As living, breathing, feeling humans, we cannot do this without eventually suffering a psychotic break. Unlike Barry Allen, Batman never indulges in the fantasy of returning to the past and righting the wrong that was done to him when his parents were taken away. This means, instead of playing the victim, Bruce Wayne became the survivor every sexually abused child wishes they could become. He separates himself from the world, becomes manically obsessed with his hobbies, and remains mentally stable. Unfortunately, this is an impossibility. A survivor cannot work the pain of the trauma away, because it will eventually surface, consume, and destroy your life from the inside out.

Healing is possible. Use this book to help move from being a hero or villain, and begin the process of healing.

Batman and the Effects Of Being a Workaholic as A Survivor of Child Sexual Abuse

As a male survivor of child sexual abuse, you may feel an overwhelming sense of shame, disgust, and self-loathing that always seems buried deep inside, waiting to rise to the surface. This feeling of isolation and feeling like a stranger in your own body can lead to an attempt to cope with your child sexual abuse through the use of maintaining control through **workaholism**. This means devoting one hundred percent of your time and energy to being perfect at the work you do, in an attempt to overwhelm the feelings of badness hidden deep inside.

Attempting to limit the bad feelings of your abuse by focusing all energy into work can best be seen in the hyperactive workaholic activities of Batman. Batman spends his days as billionaire Bruce Wayne and his nights protecting the streets of Gotham. He spends every moment of every day and night planning for every situation. He feels as though Gotham is his responsibility. He works to make up for his past. You, as a survivor of child sexual abuse, may push your ability and need to stay busy to its very extreme. You may hide behind your work and refuse to stop moving for even a moment, out of fear that the trauma of your sexual abuse may be too much to bear.

The Workaholism of Bruce Wayne That Led to the Creation of Batman

For Batman to be one of the few humans with no special powers or abilities (other than a bottomless bank account) to be considered a superhero that equals, or even surpasses, the caliber of Superman and Wonder Woman, there was an unimaginable amount of trials, training, and study involved. This consistent striving for perfection and planning for every possible scenario is what makes Batman the ideal character to understand how childhood trauma can lead to workaholism in order to suppress feelings of worthlessness, depression, sadness, and isolation. However, unlike the separate façades of Superman, the identity of billionaire playboy and business tycoon Bruce Wayne, and the protector of Gotham, Batman, are in many ways the same person. So, to understand their history, they must be examined together as one person rather than separately. While the joint nature of both Batman and Bruce Wayne is somewhat inseparable as adults, as children this was not the case. The unification of the two characters, and the development of Batman into eventual being, occurred at 10:47 p.m. on a warm summer night when Bruce was eight years old. It was at that time that Bruce Wayne lost his parents and his childhood.

On that night, Bruce Wayne's parents, Thomas and Martha Wayne, went with their son to attend a 1920s classic silent movie *The Mask of Zorro*. While walking through Park Row at the end of the movie, the Waynes were robbed at gunpoint. Thomas Wayne stepped in front of the gunman, Joe Chill, to block his wife and son from harm. As he did, the man was shot. Screaming for help as the gunman reached for her pearls, Martha was shot as well. With both parents shot and Bruce standing alone on the sidewalk, Chill ran from the scene, leaving Bruce alone to watch as his parents bled on the sidewalk and died. Orphaned, Bruce was raised by his butler, Alfred Pennyworth, with the help of Leslie Thompkins, a surgeon who worked with Thomas Wayne.

The story of Batman's origins has been told many times over the last seventy-five years with many minuet changes, but much of the story told above is what has remained constant. However, what is certain is that on the night Bruce lost his parents, Batman began his assent into being, and Bruce Wayne became merely a means for the Caped Crusader to continue his war on crime.

This assent into existence began at the age of fourteen. Until that time, Bruce remained at Wayne Manor. When he finally did leave to begin his training as Batman, he traveled the world. He began in Asia, learning from the League of Assassins before journeying to Japan, China, Nepal, Africa, and the Middle East to master all known forms of hand-to-hand combat. To better not only his body but his mind, Bruce studied at the finest institutions from the Berlin School of Science, Cambridge University, and the Sorbonne in France. At many of these schools, he stayed for only a semester or two, picking the subjects he felt he needed the most. Throughout his studies, he mastered Arabic, Chinese, Japanese, Tibetan, Eskimo, Latin, French, German, Spanish, and Kryptonese using his photographic memory. By his early twenties, Bruce returned to Wayne Manor a different man, ready to begin his war on crime in Gotham.

Once back in Gotham, he adopted the image of the Batman after seeing a bat trapped inside Wayne Manor. Below the estate is where he established his headquarters in a series of catacombs, tunnels, and multi-tiered caves known to many as the Batcave. It is here he established a research laboratory, training facility, and trophy room that could only be accessed through a hidden passage behind a grandfather clock that opens when set to 10:47.

Batman has no super abilities. He is simply a man. However, he has fought monsters, stood with gods, and accomplished the impossible. In *Superman/Batman #32* from February 2007, Alfred says this about Batman's abilities:

> *He's at his best when cornered. Faced with the possibility of death, most of us descend into the throes of panic. But not the Batman. They think he will somehow be afraid of them. Frightened by their twisted faces, contorted with evil. They don't understand that he's not seeing their faces in the struggle, but the face of the one who killed his parents. And then his own face with tears. It's what gives him the strength to face any opponent. The Batman endures because his sorrow has been channeled into a white-hot righteousness. As a child, he could only watch while his parents bled to death in the street. He refused to ever feel that hopelessness again.*

As a male survivor of child sexual abuse, your drive to fill every waking moment with work and planning to see you through the day, week, month, and well into the future is the same drive that pushes Batman to never stop fighting. In the same way that Batman sees his abuser and himself as weak and inadequate as a boy, you may view yourself and your abuse in the same way. When you may be tired, exhausted, physically and emotionally drained in whatever task you are doing, you see the face of your abuser taking away your sense of safety, joy, and childhood, in the same way Batman see the face and gun of Joe Chill.

You may also view yourself after the trauma as weak and unable to protect yourself. Thinking back to who you were and the lost, hurt, and alone boy you were in the past, you may think you never want to be that person again. So, like Batman, you take control. You plan for situations to ensure you know the outcome. You study, remain focused, keep others at a safe distance, and never stay still long enough to enjoy a victory or feel the full impact of the sadness and regret forced on you as a child. To the world you appear amazing, while on the inside you battle demons that never provide a moment's rest. This portion of the book will examine the impact of this constant need to "do" something on your feelings and your body using Batman as the archetype.

Effects of Child Sexual Abuse on Your Feelings

As a male survivor of child sexual abuse, you may think that your feelings are dangerous. Coming of age in an unstable household in which your body was violated, you may think you cannot afford to feel the full range of your terror, pain, shame, or rage, because the results would be catastrophic. You may also feel that because you were sexually abused your body is no longer safe. This means isolating your emotions and feeling like a stranger in your own body. According to *The Courage to Heal* (1992), the effects on your feelings as a male survivor of child sexual abuse may mean finding it difficult to:

- recognize your feelings
- differentiate between emotions
- express feelings
- calm down when you get upset

As a male survivor, you may also feel:

- disconnected, isolated, and alone;
- a pervasive sense of shame;

- just a few feelings, rather than a full range of emotions;
- out of control with your rage or feelings;
- confused;
- dead inside.

As a male survivor, you may also:

- be prone to depression or despair;
- struggle with anxiety or have panic attacks;
- alternate between overwhelming anxiety, fear or rage, and being numb and shutdown;
- feel agitated and on alert;
- have frequent nightmares;
- are afraid of your emotions;
- worry about going crazy;
- rarely feel pleasure, relaxation, or joy.

Because of these feelings of isolation, often survivors:

- aren't aware of the messages their bodies give them or don't respond to the messages
- feel numb or disconnected from physical sensations
- are on high alert for danger
- are unable to feel physically safe

In many ways, you are similar to Batman and his feelings of weakness, shame, and fear over his inability to prevent the death of his parents. Bruce Wayne is ashamed of his failure as a boy to stop the murder of his parent. He views himself as weak, vulnerable, and helpless in that moment. Since then, he refuses to ever feel that sense of fear and weakness again. You, as a survivor, may have a pervasive sense of shame because of you perceived sense of weakness and inability to prevent your sexual abuse. It's for this reason you may feel pleasure remotely and rarely, if ever relax and enjoy life.

Instead of shame for being unable to prevent the death of your parents, you may have a sense of shame for the undeniable truth that you had no way of preventing your sexual abuse. The pleasure and joy you feel in life may be minimal, in the same ways that Batman and Bruce Wayne limit the emotions they feel through the constant work they do to plan for every possible conflict and never feel the sense of fear they felt on the night of their parents' death. This idea of being a workaholic and its effect on minimizing feelings can best be seen in *Detective Comics #574*.

My Beginning . . . And My Probable End . . .

Feelings govern who we are and how we react to situations within and out of our control. Without the proper expression of our feelings of grief, shame, and pain, it not only leads to a world of isolation, but it can damage the feelings of others who want to be included in your life. This issue explores the isolation and loneliness created by trauma and how your lack of expression of feelings can not only hurt you as a male survivor of sexual abuse, but those closest to you.

The story begins with rain. Outside the Thomas Wayne Memorial Clinic, two street thugs discuss whether to rob the medical facility to get some cash and a fix. Before they can make up their minds, Batman falls from the sky and kicks in the door. A skinny white woman with short white hair runs toward the door with a bat before stopping in her tracks, seeing Batman standing in the door, drenched in rain, holding the limp body of Robin, Jason Todd, pleading with the little old woman known as Leslie Thompkins to help him.

As is true with all Batman comics, the use of color is a large factor in the way the story is told. Issue #574 is no different. The use of blue, black, green, yellow, red, and white tell a tale all their own as the story unfolds.

Batman explains how the Mad Hatter shot Jason four times with a .38 caliber. Leslie, the only doctor on duty, dressed in all white, calls the Dark Knight 'Bruce' instead of Batman. As they speak and wheel Jason toward the operating room, she speaks candidly, never second guessing her words, biting tone, and angered glances as she tells Batman that Jason has a faint heartbeat. Before taking the Boy Wonder away in an attempt to save his life, she tells Batman to pray.

Alone in the darkness of the waiting room, Batman sits with his eyes closed, waiting for Leslie to return. As he waits, he remembers his parents and the night they were killed. As these memories transpire and the flashback begins, the colors of the comic change to images of red, black, and orange. Here, Martha Wayne looks down with a smile on her face and asks her son, who is holding the hand of both his parents, if he enjoyed the movie. The scene quickly turns from one of joy to sadness, as a passerby asks Thomas Wayne for a cigarette. Telling the man he does not smoke, the passerby takes out a gun. Within seconds, young Bruce Wayne witnesses his father and then his mother being shot dead by a thief attempting to take his mother's pearls.

After shooting both his parents, the thief points the gun at Bruce. He tells the boy, "Stop lookin' at me. Stop it!"

Bruce points his finger and repeats over and over again, "They're dead. They're dead." The thief panics as Bruce begins to hit the murderer while continuing to repeat, "They're dead! They're dead! You did it! You!" To get away, he hits Bruce with the butt of the gun, runs away, and throws the gun in the bushes as he flees.

It's in these moments that Bruce begins to lose the feelings of joy and happiness he once had, in the same you, as a male survivor of child sexual abuse, lost your sense of joy and childhood following the trauma. Instead, his happiness is replaced with anger, shame, regret, and sadness as Gotham Morgue carried away the bodies of his parents. Alone and emotionally lost, Leslie takes Bruce in her arms and holds him as he cries.

When the flashback comes to an end, color returns to the comic and Leslie reappears in the waiting room. She tells Batman she did all she could and that Jason will probably survive. As Batman and Leslie begin to argue the cause of Jason's injuries, Batman tells Leslie:

I did it for him, for the boy I saved from a life of crime, for the boy who saved himself. I didn't choose Jason for my work. He was chosen by it as I was chosen to do the work I was born to. My life's work, work that became my life.

Later, Batman remembers the night his parents died and his first night with Leslie. As the colors of the comic change to gray, black, red, orange, and yellow There are no words for two pages. Instead, it's a series of pictures explaining Bruce's rage, regret, and sadness. The young Bruce Wayne sneaks out of bed and enters Crown Hill Cemetery. Inside, an angel extends its wings in the moonlight as Bruce kneels and cries with sadness. In the next panel, Bruce's sadness is transformed into rage as he balls his hand into a fist, grits his teeth, and opens his eyes with defiance at the angel, as tears continue to stream down his face. Finally, he screams in the shadow of angel, which creates the symbolic image of bat wings and pointed ears. It's here that Bruce Wayne represses his feelings, refusing to acknowledge his trauma as he begins to become a workaholic to drown his emotions. You, as a male survivor, may recall a similar instance when you made the decision to work instead of feel.

The flashback continues as he visits the spot of his parent's death. Chalk outlines the places where his parents laid dying on the bloodstained sidewalk beneath the illumination of a streetlight. Bruce turns away from the scene with an expression of anger, as he digs in the bushes to find the gun thrown away by the murderer. Bruce stares at the gun with numb hatred, puts it inside his coat, and runs into the darkness. As he runs from the scene of the crime, he no longer feels the sadness, depression, and mourning over the loss of his parents, innocence, and childhood, in the same way you may have literally and figuratively run away from the scene of your abuse by running away from home, leaving for college, and moving to a different city or state. When this occurred, the only emotions that remained for Bruce, and yourself as a survivor, are shame, regret, and hatred of your own weakness.

As the flashback continues, Bruce works relentlessly to never feel weak again. Leslie and Alfred watch with concern as Bruce reads *The Adventures of Sherlock Holmes* with stern resolve, as reality returns to Batman telling Leslie he had his work. He explains that in college all he needed was knowledge and solitude, which further repressed his emotions.

As the panels transition back to the orange, blue, gray, and red of the past, Batman tells Leslie:

> *I needed two things out of college—knowledge and solitude. The second was simple. I'd show up on campus reeking of money and superiority. Before long, I had to pay anyone to spend time with me. Knowledge was a little tougher. However, if I planned to avenge my parents, I knew it could never be connected with Bruce Wayne, so Bruce became a thoroughly bored, utterly useless student who showed up at classes when he felt like it, which wasn't often. I studied on my own, of course, but when I found a problem I couldn't quite lick. Its solution was an education in itself. I'd disguise my features. No one seemed to think it odd that Bruce Wayne should take an interest in theatre arts and become a visiting student, asking questions of such insight that the professor nearly gave me a scholarship. Of course, even that didn't work all the time. Once in a while I'd stumble onto something the professor said was too advanced, so I'd do a little extra credit work at night. The fact that I wasn't looking to better my grades wouldn't have cut any ice with the Dean, had I been caught. So, I made sure I wasn't. The entire experience was another education in itself. I wouldn't have missed it for anything.*

These panels reveal a lot about Bruce Wayne's past. His need to better himself while limiting his emotions explains how he became the Batman of Gotham City. It also explains how you may be able to relate to the workaholic you have become by limiting your feelings. When reality returns to the comic, Leslie even comments about how lonely his life seemed and if he wants the same kind of life for Jason. Batman responds:

> *I remember what I was like. I suppose I was lonely. I don't want Jason to grow up as I did. I didn't know what to do, didn't know how to fight my war until my youth was gone. I wanted to give Jason an outlet for his rage, wanted him to expunge his anger and get on with his life.*

The final flashback reveals Bruce alone, studying and becoming Batman with an expression of consternation, while Jason played baseball and defeated villains as Robin with an expression of sheer joy.

The story ends with Jason making a full recovery and the two continuing their war on crime, but this comic explains and perpetuates the need for males who suffer trauma to self-medicate rather than seek help. Throughout the comic, it is revealed that Batman only trusted himself to heal the void created by the loss of his parents, while forcing Jason to do the same. He pushed down his feelings of isolation and shame as Bruce Wayne, while expunging his anger and hatred as the Batman. Unfortunately, too many male survivors do the same. According to Men's Health Table in 2009, treatment for depression is least common among men. Of the adult males between the ages of 18-25 who suffered a major depressive episode in 2009, 37.9 percent received treatment, 56.2 percent of adult males between 26-49 received treatment, and 76.1 percent of adult males 50 and older received treatment. This means young adults males are more likely to experience depression without services, making men four times more likely to die of suicide than woman.

If this comic teaches you anything about being a male survivor of child sexual abuse, it's that you can't be like Batman. Limiting and suppressing your feelings leads to severe depression that can only be cured through counseling and therapy. Without this help, you hurt the Leslie Thompkins who try to be there when you're in need of them the most, or the Jason Todds who look up to you as a father figure and emulate your actions and beliefs. Being a male survivor means acknowledging your weakness, experiencing the full range of your emotions, and having the courage to break the stereotype of the stoic male and seek healing.

Effects Of Child Sexual Abuse on Your Body

When you were sexually abused, the freedom of feeling as though you owned your own body was taken away. The abuse made it so that you could no longer feel safe in your own body, because it's a place where frightening and painful things happen. It's for this reason you may ignore your body or be on high alert. According to *Courage to Heal*, as a male survivor, you may have a hard time:

- appreciating and accepting your body
- feeling at home in your skin
- being fully present in your body
- experiencing a full range of feelings
- experiencing your body as a unified whole

As a male survivor of sexual abuse, you may have:

- hurt yourself or abused your body
- misused or are addicted to alcohol or drugs
- have an eating disorder
- have physical illnesses that may be connected to your abuse
- feel as though you sometimes leave your body
- don't feel pleasure in physical activities

Often as a male survivor you:

- aren't aware of the messages your body gives you or don't respond to these messages
- mistrust or blame your body
- feel numb or disconnected from physical sensations
- startle easily and have a hard time calming down

- are often on high alert for danger
- are unable to relax or feel physically safe

As a male survivor of sexual abuse, you may ignore the messages your body sends you, such as signals of pain, discomfort, or exhaustion. This is not uncommon for survivors of child sexual abuse. To survive your trauma, you may have had to dissociate your mind from your body and become numb to the signals sent to your brain. This means possibly pushing your body to its limits and not knowing you are on the verge of collapse until it's too late.

These traits can also be seen in Batman in a few ways. Bruce Wayne pushes his body to the very limit every day, after doing the same each night as Batman. He rarely sleeps, never stops training, and prepares his mind and body for every situation. In each instance, he either ignores or does not feel the signals of pain or fear his body sends him. You, as a male survivor, may fear, mistrust, or blame your body for the trauma you suffered. Like Batman, your senses are on high alert, unaware of messages your body sends, and you are unable to relax or feel physically safe.

These qualities make Batman an ideal character to help you understand how the effects of your sexual trauma have stunted your ability to feel and understand the signals of your body. There is no better Batman comic to illustrate this than *Batman #497* (1993) and the breaking of Batman's back by Bane.

Broken Bat

Bane is arguably one of the most ruthless villains of Batman's Rogue Gallery. He is intelligent, ruthless, only cares about acquiring more power, and uses a serum known as "Venom" to give him super strength. *Batman #497* reveals Bane's ruthlessness and ingenuity as a villain capable of bringing down the Batman (and Christopher Noland choosing him as a major character in the third film of his epic Batman trilogy, *The Dark Knight Rises*) when the story begins with Bane standing inside Wayne Manor, staring at the face of shocked Bruce Wayne emerging from the Batcave wearing a robe over his Batman costume. His cowl is off and Alfred lies on the ground unconscious.

In these first few pages of the comic, Bruce looks rough, to say the very least. He has a five o'clock shadow, his hair is disheveled, and he's in a gaudy silk robe in true rich playboy style. However, what it truly startling as a reader and lover of his often stoic and unfeeling expressions is the look of shock, confusion, and fear. These emotions are never shown by the calculative and methodical Batman, but to see behind the mask of Batman, and even the façade of aloof playboy billionaire Bruce Wayne, made the pages more horrific, real, and fearful for the safety of the world's greatest detective.

For three pages, readers are shown a different side of Bob Kane's Batman, as the hero and the villain stand in Wayne Manor, discussing the fight about to happen like gentlemen. Common roles of hero and villain have been reversed. Bane stands firm, confident, and prepared for what is to come, while Wayne attempts to piece together not only how he never saw this coming, but how he's going to fight a battle he knows he can't win.

Finally, on page five the fearless fighting Caped Crusader returns as he throws off his robe to reveal flexed and tense muscles ready for battle. He pulls on his cowl to truly become Batman, grits his teeth, and lunges over the body of Alfred to attack Bane head on. Unfortunately, the usual hand-to-hand combat, where equally formidable foes fight and meet hands and fists with appropriate blocks and counter moves, does not take place. Instead, the battle is one-sided. Batman never lands a punch. Instead, Bane backhands the hero across the face, sending him flying across the room into the wall of his mansion. The fight moves throughout Wayne Manor, destroying every piece of furniture and priceless antique in their way, and into the Batcave, also destroying priceless trophies and costumes of fallen heroes collected throughout the years, before ending with Batman battered, beaten, bleeding, and barely conscious with a broken back, as Bane walks away unharmed.

While the fight between Bane and Batman is epic, as a male survivor of child sexual abuse, this is not the reason for including this comic as a guide for recovery. Instead, it was chosen to help in understanding how you may ignore your body's signals until it is too late. To understand how Batman, like you, may often ignore the signals of pain and fatigue until you can no longer function, you have to understand what took place that led up to the battle between Batman and Bane.

Throughout the comic, Bane reveals to Batman (while knocking him from one side of the room to the other) how he released all the criminals Batman put away at Arkham Asylum (this is a jail for the criminally insane). When Bane did this, he knew Batman would put all of his time and energy into capturing and defeating each villain that was set free. With each blow from Bane, Batman remembers the endless battles between himself and his enemies. He remembers each punch and battle over the endless weeks, wearing him down to nothing until the fight with Bane left him a hollow shell with a fraction of his abilities and strength. Batman's words of defeat and sheer exhaustion may sound familiar to you as a male survivor who ignores the needs of their body and pushes themselves to the brink because of the impact of the trauma of their sexual abuse on their psyche.

This time I'm doomed. Pushing too hard too long, facing the madness of too many masks, bearing the brunt of too much violence. too much pain. Already burned down and out from both ends and every angle. Battered, bashed, and scarred from a thousand cuts and blows. Tottering on brittle bones and lurching through vertigo for months now, ears buzzing and ringing, everything too bright and glittery, even in the dark. Too much punishment, overwhelming odds, passing blood for weeks, racing for death my whole life. Every muscle sluggish and trembling, all strength stretched and sapped, washed in weakness, mired in slow motion panic for helplessness. And through it all, no sleep, no rest, even when movement itself was impossible. Nothing but the mind's desperate urge to get off the floor and strike back, even when every uphill effort is wasted and futile. Reality itself smashed and splintered, like the rude death of an impossible dream, awakening again and again to nothing but agony, relentless and repeated. And then the crowning horror of shattered Arkham spilling its mad guts into the long dark night of hopeless horror. A legion of crazed killers loosed on Gotham, too many, too much to fight. And the fall, so great, pride no longer an asset, only prelude to a fall, leaving me drained and depleted , utterly empty. But still they loomed and lunged from the dark. laughing demons with bad intent bearing pain and nothing more, chipping away at whatever was left, wearing me down toward nothing and nowhere. Vertigo . Whirling out of control now, time distorted, images flashing. Then and now a confused blur, every shock and concussion the same, each devastating and all adding up to one long plunge into hell. Nightmarish. Never-ending. Garish and bizarre. Insanity too stark to suffer or surmount.

While this is the internal dialogue of a fictional hero falling from grace as his body fails him and is pummeled by a heartless villain, many of his words may reverberate with familiarity. Some of these same words and sentences may sound like some of the words you say to yourself when thinking and expecting yourself to do more than you can. You may also say these same things to yourself when having a panic or anxiety attack and try to talk yourself out of it as you tumble to your lowest. As a male survivor of child sexual abuse, you may view yourself as more than human in your ability to endure pain and stress, while feeling as though you are less than human and undeserving of remorse, love, forgiveness, or kindness because of your trauma.

As a survivor, you have to remember the same thing Batman sometimes forgets. You are human, and no matter how you were sexual abused as a child, you did not deserve it and you're allowed to be loved. There's no need for forgiveness because you did nothing wrong. Kindness and remorse from others is not a sign of weakness. Instead, it's simply a feeling you and others are allowed to experience when stressed, anxious, sad, or depressed. You, as a male survivor, *have* been through hell and you *are* allowed to feel weakness or exhaustion. The fact that you are still breathing and living is a miracle itself. Be kind to yourself and don't break your back attempting to do more than humanly possible. This is not saying you should not push yourself to do more and become more, but know and accept that you can and do have limits. Be more, but know you are mortal. This does not make you weak, but stronger in knowing what you can and cannot achieve.

As you progress toward healing, keep the Serenity Prayer in your thoughts: "God, grant me the security to accept the things I cannot, the courage to change the things I can, and the wisdom to know the difference."

Effects Of Child Sexual Abuse on Your Sexuality

The ideal male image is present throughout every issue of Superman, Shazam, Green Lantern, Flash, and countless others. However, there is one issue that is never discussed on its pages written and designed for young adults, but which affects the life of male sexual abuse survivors everyday of their lives: sex. Although your feelings of being an alien in your own body are true, there are also negative assumptions about how the body should look and behave sexually that apply to both genders and many different races. Although your sexuality was stripped away because of your abuse, unfortunately there is no male hero, villain, or comic in the DC universe I feel comfortable using to help you understand the impact this trauma has had on your life sexually, but it's a part of understanding your trauma that must be discussed.

Sexuality is a large part of an individual's personality. This is one of the primary reasons rape is such a heinous and detrimental crime. Stripping away an individual's sexuality strips away their identity, leaving them to wonder who they are and where they fit into society. Your sexual abuse as a male survivor is no different. Because of your sexual abuse as a child you may wonder:

- Am I still a man if I feel uncomfortable wanting or having sex?

- How do I explain to my partner my negative mental and physical reactions to having sex or being intimate?

This is because the negative assumptions of what it means to be a "true man" are representative and woven throughout every thread of our society, including the comics and heroes you have grown to love and represented throughout this book. The "perfect" male body of broad shoulders, six-pack abs, well-defined legs, and a perfectly symmetrical face, absent of blemishes, appears on every color-filled page of a graphic novel. While this image is true for our heroes, it is not always true for the villains who are sometimes drawn skinny, pale, weak, and homoerotic. These traits can be seen in the pale skin of the Joker, the skinny body and tight-fitted clothing of Shade, and many others. These perpetuated stereotypes lead to false expectations of what it means to be normal. This means that as a male survivor when it comes to sex you may, according to *The Courage to Heal*:

- feel disconnected when you have sex;

- go through sex numb or in panic;

- use sex to meet needs that aren't sexual;

- avoid sex, or seek sex you really don't want;

- feel that your worth is primarily sexual;

- feel conflicted when you experience desire or sexual pleasure;

- need to control everything about sex to feel safe;

- experience flashbacks of your abuse while making love;

- feel confused about whether you want to have sex.

As a male survivor, you may also have trouble:

- saying no to sex that you don't want

- accepting nurturing or closeness that isn't sexual

- staying present when making love

- being emotionally close and sexual at the same time (with the same person)

Some male survivors:

- think sex is disgusting or that you're disgusting for enjoying it;
- are turned on by violent, sadistic, or incestuous fantasies;
- engage in sex that repeats aspects of your abuse;
- have continued to be sexually abused;
- use sex as a way to exert power and control;
- have been sexually abusive to others.

The effects and thoughts of your sexual abuse listed above mean your view of sex as a source of love and intimacy may be skewed. Attempts at engaging in sexual activity may produce triggers of the trauma you suffered as a child. These triggers, which many times occur without warning, may send you into panic and anxiety attacks. In some cases, this may lead you to attempt to avoid having sex. The perpetuation of the hyper-masculine identity may force you to feel as though you should have an unquenchable desire for sex. These lessons taught as a boy and instilled in you as a man may lead to an addiction to sex where the false façade you carry of needing and wanting sex may lead to one hollow and emotionless encounter after another. Your trauma as a child may lead to an addiction of pornography, phone sex, internet sex, and even violent and abusive sexual encounters. The addictions stem from the sexual abuse you suffered as a child, and the false lessons of a "true man" taught to you as a boy cannot be unlearned as an adult without the proper help and healing of therapy, reflection, and meditation.

Chapter Five
Captain Marvel:
The Dissociated Boy

"It's not that I can't be mean. I could cuss a bunch and kill all the bad guys and stuff. But . . . look I can't even drive yet. I don't have a bank account. I can't vote or drink and I haven't been to college. I don't understand everything. So until I do, I'm gonna use the power I've got to do the right thing. Call me a wussy if you want, I'm just a boy trying to be a good man."

—Captain Marvel/Billy Batson

Captain Marvel and the Effects Of Dissociation as A Male Survivor Of Child Sexual Abuse

As a male survivor of child sexual abuse, you may have taught yourself that your body cannot be trusted and is not safe for you to enjoy and feel free to live in. This is because the safety and security of living in your own body was taken away when you were sexually abused as a child. The fear of being violated again, even as an adult, may lead you to sometimes disconnect from your body. The ability to separate your mind from your body and the emotions and feelings it causes you to experience is a result of coping with pain you were forced to endure. When you were a child, you may not have been able to physically escape your abuse, so you emotionally and psychically separated from your abuse. This process is known as dissociation, and it gave you the ability to endure tremendous pain that was impossible to endure without the ability to separate your mind from your body. When a survivor dissociates from their body they:

- may not feel pleasure in physical activities
- aren't aware of messages their bodies give them
- feel numb or disconnected from physical sensations
- are often on high alert for danger
- unable to relax or feel physically safe

As a child, this coping strategy may have been essential to your survival. However, as an adult, dissociation can become a habit and create problems when dealing with threatening situations. In some cases, it can lead to dissociative identity disorder. This occurs when there is no way to physically escape pain, which is otherwise intolerable, and creating new selves, or alternate personalities, to separate from the abuse and withstand the trauma. While healing from DID may be more complicated than healing from simple dissociation, it can be accomplished. Although the journey is difficult, the first step is understanding the trauma you suffered as a child to heal from it.

To fully understand dissociation and its effects, we can turn to the mightiest mortal, Captain Marvel, otherwise known as Shazam.

Captain Marvel and Dissociation

Captain Marvel came into existence in the 1940s *Whiz Comics #2*, "Introducing Captain Marvel," with a young boy in his early

63

teens named Billy Batson. The comic explains the death of Billy's parents, and being driven from the home of his uncle who stole the money willed to the boy by his parents after their passing. To survive, the young boy sells newspapers to provide for himself. Alone in the rain, homeless, and sleeping in the subway station, a man in a black trench coat and black hat, pulled low to only reveal his white eyes, tells Billy to follow him. Fortunately, modern stranger danger did not apply to the beliefs of young boys in the 1940s, so Billy followed.

The shadowed figure leads the boy to a subway car decorated with weird shapes and colors. When the two enter the car, they are the only passengers. When the car comes to a stop, the two exit and walk down a long cavern lit with torches. Along the walls are carvings of statues. Above the statues is written "The Seven Deadly Enemies of Man." The bottom of each statue is labeled with a sin. When they reach the end of the cavern, Billy is greeted by an old white man with a white beard, dressed in all white, sitting on a marble throne. The man tells Billy that his name is Shazam. He explains that for three thousand years he has used his wisdom, strength, stamina, power, courage, and speed to battle the forces of evil. Shazam tells Billy he has been watching the boy for a long time, and because the wizard is old, Billy will be his successor and become the mightiest man in the world, Captain Marvel. All Billy has to do is speak the name of the wizard and he will be endowed with the powers of the gods:

> **S**olomon's wisdom
>
> **H**ercules's Strength
>
> **A**tlas's stamina
>
> **Z**eus's power
>
> **A**chilles' courage
>
> **M**ercury's speed

In that instant that the boy speaks the acronym, Shazam, with a flash of lightening Billy Batson transforms from a skinny young boy into the full-bodied grown hero Captain Marvel, wearing a red uniform with a yellow sash, with yellow lightning bolt in the center of his chest, yellow boots, yellow bracelets, and a white-and-yellow cape covering his left shoulder. Once transformed, the hero is told by the old wizard to defend the poor and helpless while righting wrongs. He's also told that to transform from Captain Marvel back into Billy Batson, all he has to do is speak the word *Shazam* for a second time. When he does, he becomes Billy while breaking the thread of a massive block of granite hanging over the head of the old wizard, crushing him flat.

The lesson to be taken away from Captain Marvel (Shazam) and Billy Batson is that as a male survivor of sexual abuse you dissociate from your body as an adult. Also, as a survivor, you may feel a lot like Billy, a boy trapped inside the body of a man, with powers you don't understand and feelings you believe you are not allowed to express because society views them as inappropriate and meant only for children.

This dissociation can be seen in Captain Marvel and Billy Batson. Although there have been many reincarnations of Captain Marvel over the years, some things have remained consistent. One of those being that when Billy is in danger or in need of help, he says the magic word, "Shazam," and becomes Captain Marvel. In the same way you may separate your thoughts, feelings, and actions from your body when threatened, Billy dissociates from his body to become someone new who is able to take on the dangers the young boy cannot.

This dissociation of Billy Batson into Captain Marvel can best be understood and help you understand your own dissociation in the 1974 comic in which Superman battles a Captain Marvel from an alternate dimension who has turned evil and is known as Captain Thunder rather than Captain Marvel.

Make Way for Captain Thunder!

Sometimes being a survivor of child sexual abuse means losing contact with your body, forgetting actions and conversations that were too difficult to bear, and possibly creating different personalities to navigate the stresses of the real world through dissociation. To understand its effects on you as a survivor of child sexual abuse, it's best to examine the effects of dissociation of a character very similar to Billy Batson in *Superman #276*, "Make Way for Captain Thunder."

It's important to note that during this time DC was battling in court with Whiz Comics over the use of the name Captain Marvel. As the rights of the name and characters were being sorted out, DC decided that rather than writing a story involving Billy Batson and Captain Marvel, they wrote a comic with a young boy named Willie Fawcett and the hero Captain Thunder. The differences between the two heroes are subtle but noticeable. Rather than Captain Thunder being endowed with magical powers from the wizard Shazam, he receives his powers from an ancient Native American shaman. While both have names that are acronyms, Captain Thunder's has been altered to match the powers of Native American culture and their belief in a connection to nature. Rather than the powers of the Greek gods, Willie Fawcett has the power of THUNDER:

> Tornado . . . power
>
> Hare . . . speed
>
> Uncas . . . bravery
>
> Nature . . . wisdom
>
> Diamond . . . toughness
>
> Eagle . . . flight
>
> Ram . . . tenacity

Although there are other changes between the two heroes, the fact that Willie Fawcett transforms into the hero Captain Thunder in times of danger remains the same, making the negative effects of dissociation apparent throughout the comic.

The story begins with Willie appearing in the alley of a metropolis with no memory of how he got there or even where he is. He walks throughout the city, attempting to make sense of why and how the city he knew had changed in appearance, name, and design. While walking the streets, Willie comes face-to-face with an armored car robbery. Seeing danger and knowing he can help, Willie rubs the buckle of his belt, and calls out "Thunder!" When he does, Captain Thunder appears. However, rather than attempt to stop the robbery, he assists the robbers in getting away with the armored car and fighting Superman. The battle between the two heroes ends when Captain Thunder throws the armored car at the Man of Steel and transforms back into Willie Fawcett. When this happens, Willie has no idea how he got there, no memory of the battle with Superman, and no knowledge of his sudden transformation to the side of evil.

As the story continues, Willie begins to understand what has happened and how to return home, but not before another epic battle between Captain Thunder and Superman.

When the battle ends, Captain Thunder goes away and Willie takes his place. However, the boy still cannot remember fighting Superman and wants the fighting to stop. He wants to remember his actions and begs to return home. By the end of the story, Captain Thunder realizes his actions have become evil, understands what has happened to alter the connection between Willie and himself, and discovers how to return both him and Willie to their proper dimension.

While this story does not involve the true Captain Marvel and Billie Batson, it reveals the true nature of dissociation and the effects it can have on you as a male survivor of child sexual abuse. As a survivor, there may be moments you leave your body. Triggers such as certain smells, sounds, or textures cause you to return to a memory from your past or simply vanish. These instances can be harmless, but other instances may be more severe. Hours of your day may be lost when you finally wake up from your dissociative experience, unsure of where you are or what you have done, in the same way Willie had no memory of Captain Marvel's actions. The only cure is to seek help and healing through therapy. Then you can begin to recognize the disorder and how to combat its effects. It's difficult, but it can be done. You can regain all dissociated pieces and parts of your life.

Real Men Don't . . .

Society teaches men, in the same way it teaches women, what it means to be a "real man," through the words individuals use, the images individuals see, and all things in between. Men, like women, are told what is socially acceptable from the moment of birth, and they are given either blue or pink hats and socks. As both genders mature, hints of what is acceptable throughout society are sprinkled in words said by parents in houses, relatives at reunions, teachers in classrooms, and kids on playgrounds. Words of praise and shame such as: "my little princess," "you're my big man," "cute," "handsome," "you throw like a girl," "don't be a pussy," "fag," and "man up."

Over time, images in magazines, movies, commercials, and even books inform both genders that the most accepted females are those with tanned, white skin, large breasts, small waists, big butts, and toned legs, while the most accepted men are those that have six-pack abs, broad shoulders, muscular legs, and, of course, white, tanned skin. Soon, as adults, men and women have an unconscious understanding of what it means to be a real man or woman. Unfortunately, these impossible expectations can have detrimental effects for both men and women, especially for men who have suffered sexual abuse as children.

Captain Marvel fits the stereotype of what it means to be a perfect man and the falsehoods it portrays. Billy Batson transforms from a preteen into an adult man with the flash of a bolt of lightning. Physically, he represents all aspects of what it means to be a "real man." He's strong, handsome, and somewhat mysterious. However, on the inside he is a little boy who thinks and, in many ways, behaves like a child. As a male survivor, you may try to live up to the image society portrays as representing a true man, while on the inside you feel like a trapped, scared little boy, blindly making his way through a world of adults.

There is no such thing as a perfect man. Unfortunately, men who have been sexually abused as children strive for perfection to live up to impossible stereotypes, and they hurt themselves in the process. To overcome the trauma of child sexual abuse, you may find understanding the boy locked inside the body of the "world's mightiest mortal" may help to understand the effects of losing your own childhood and why locking away your inner boy may have been protection from the harsh reality you were forced to endure.

Where Dreams End

In essence, Captain Marvel is a boy trapped inside the body of an adult male. Captain Marvel works as a superhero because of the attraction of reading the adventures of a hero fighting crime and opposing villains with the strength of Superman while holding onto an optimistic view of the world through the eyes of a child. Life has yet to harden the view of the child and change the way in which he interacts and approaches situations. It's for this reason the wizard Shazam chose Billy Batson and not a grown man to wield the power of the gods to become the world's mightiest mortal. It's true he has seen and experienced hardships, such as being homeless, but the impact of experiencing continuous hardships time after time would affect the innocence he has and the way in which he views the world.

The appeal of Captain Marvel's innocence and optimism can best be understood in *The Power of Shazam #1-2* (1995), "Things Change" and "The Arson Fiend." Here, Billy transforms into Captain Marvel to attend a social engagement and is approached by a blond bombshell named Beautia. When this occurs, he has no idea how to approach the situation, as he sweats bullets and she looks longingly for more than just an autograph.

The same childlike innocence and belief in the need to uphold a belief in the goodness of people over the possibility of their evil nature occurs in *L.E.G.I.O.N. '91 #31*, "Where Dreams End." In this adventure, Captain Marvel refuses to fight the "intergalactic main man," Lobo, after crashing into the hot head, causing him to spill his beer. Lobo, being the hardcore intergalactic rocker who stigmatizes the archetype of what it means to be a man, solves problems with his fists and punches Captain Marvel into a wall, throws a drink into his face, and has his seat pulled from beneath him.

Throughout all this abuse, Captain Marvel does not throw a single punch. Instead, after sipping on a milkshake in an intergalactic bar, he states, "Violence, if it's to be employed at all, can only be as a means of absolute last resort!"

It's not until Captain Marvel hears pleas of help coming from the bathroom and finds a man stuffed inside a toilet for no other reason than being at the wrong place at the wrong time that he takes action. When Marvel sees this injustice, he calls Lobo a bully and punches the white-skinned villain in the face. It's this sense of justice and right over might that allows Billy to guide Marvel like a compass toward equality and fairness when other heroes seem to waiver.

What can be learned as a male survivor of child sexual abuse is that the younger version of who you are is trapped inside in the same way Captain Marvel has Billy Batson. However, while Billy's sense of honesty and righteousness appears unwavering, yours may not. As a boy, you may have been told to behave in a certain way, to follow the "boy code" and not cry, never show any emotion besides anger or happiness, and to keep the pain you have bottled on the inside until it goes away. Over time, these lessons taught as boys became rules governing how to behave as a man. They guide actions and affect men negatively, in the same way Billy Batson guides Captain Marvel positively.

These lessons appear throughout society, and even in the comics and heroes you read about on the page or see on the silver screen. These lessons teach young boys who grow into men to not seek help or express their feelings, leading to self-medication and suicide. These lessons became rules for men and boys of sexual abuse, making them reluctant to seek support when dealing with trauma. It's for this reason that only 28.8 percent of men receive treatment according to Men's Health Table. This leads to young boys coping with sexual abuse through alcohol, drugs, and suicide,

70

and men becoming four to eighteen times more likely to kill themselves, according to the Center for Disease Control's statistics in 2009.

Without the proper help and healing from your sexual abuse, this idea of being a perfect man can change your view and how you interact with the world. Real men do not have to have six-pack abs, broad shoulders, and tanned, white skin. Real men can have a potbelly, thinning hair, and be Asian. Real men can be geeks, jocks, homosexual, and anything else they choose to be or are born as. These real men are not perfect, because perfect does not exist. However, these different shades of real mean make real fathers and husbands who change the idea of real and fake in the partners they love and the children they raise. It's these men who are the heroes and who you can become, no matter the nature of your abuse. Trust that you can be who you wish to be, heal from the trauma of your past, and become more than the archetype of a superhero. Become real.

Chapter Six
Aquaman: Trauma and Its Effects on Family Relationships

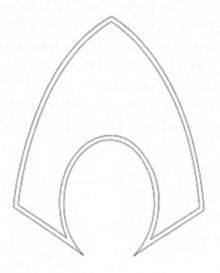

"There's an ancient wisdom I should have heeded long ago if only I had recognized its truth applies as much to me as to all men. True happiness is found along a middle road. There lies the balance and the harmony with reason and emotion not at war but hand in hand."

—*Aquaman Special, Vol. 1 No. 1*

Effects of Child Sexual Abuse on Family Relationships

According to RAINN, 38 percent of perpetrators of abuse were friends or acquaintances of the victim, 28 percent were intimate partners, and 7 percent were relatives. This means individuals being sexually abused, especially as children, are being victimized by someone they know. These can be neighbors, friends of the family, aunt, uncles, or babysitters. When this abuse occurs and is possibly discovered by members of the family, it can be devastating. Occurrences of incest can especially create strain on family relationships, when members of the family and close friends who were meant to protect children in their care instead become a source of pain and abuse. The safety, honesty, and openness that is woven throughout the fabric of healthy families is replaced with secrecy, isolation, and fear. As a male survivor of child sexual abuse, you unfortunately may have had to deal with these emotions by taking on adult responsibilities at an early age. You may also have felt that family members were unreliable and possibly a source of danger. According to *The Courage to Heal,* as a male survivor of child sexual abuse you may:

- have strained or difficult relationships with family members;
- feel crazy, invalidated, or depressed when you visit your family;
- have been rejected by your family;
- not feel safe in your family;
- continue to deal with belittling, hostile, or abusive treatment;
- be alienated or completely estranged from family members.

In many families where there has been sexual abuse:

- the sexual abuse has not been talked about or acknowledged
- incest is denied or minimized
- the survivor is told to "forgive and forget" or "let the past be in the past"
- the needs of the abuser are put ahead of the needs of the survivor

- the survivor becomes the family scapegoat; all the family's problems are blamed on them

- family members aren't supportive

In some families incest still goes on. Sexual abuse in families can be especially hard to manage and understand because of the mixed emotions that accompany the way in which you may interact with your abuser. The sexual abuse you suffered may cause you to feel anger and sadness for the trauma you suffered as a child, while at the same time it may mix with feelings of love, joy, happiness, and even admiration when recalling memories of good times. This bombardment of conflicting emotions can cause you to feel as though you are crazy, while also causing you to feel sadness, depression, and anxiety over the loss or continued dysfunction of your family.

You may also feel an obligation to do "what's right" for the family, rather than seek help and healing for yourself because of a false belief that family always comes first and that men don't show their emotions. As you begin to confront and understand the nature of your sexual abuse as a child, the fear of hurting or ripping apart your family may outweigh your own needs. However, over time, the idea of the family you want and the reality of the family you have will cause eventual self-destruction if it's not addressed.

Finally, you may still have interactions with your abuser, causing you to feel depression and anxiety with each meeting. Understanding and navigating the complexity of family relationships and the trauma you suffered can be confusing, and is not easy, but it can be accomplished. Dissecting the different relationships and interactions of the superhero Aquaman and his Aquafamily may help you understand how trauma can affect family relationships.

Aquaman and the Effects of Trauma on Family Relationships

As a male survivor of child sexual abuse, you were abused at a young age when you were weak and unable to defend yourself. Coming to terms with this may be difficult as an adult, but not impossible. To do so means moving toward healing, knowing there was nothing you could have done to prevent the abuse, and holding your abuser (no matter who they are) accountable for their actions. To accomplish these tasks, you must state that you were abused, relive the experience (no matter how difficult or painful it may be), and transcend from being a victim to becoming a survivor by revealing the nature of your sexual abuse. However, if the sexual abuse you suffered was caused by a member of your family, and stating the nature of your abuse reveals incidences of incest, it can create tension in family relationships that you may feel you caused.

Revealing the nature of your abuse to family, friends, and loved ones takes a remarkable amount of strength, courage, and healing, which takes place over an extended period of time. One reason may be because the nature of your sexual abuse may not be believed by members of your family if it involves incest. Your family may tell you to not speak of your abuse, to let it go, let the past stay in the past, or that the abuse was your fault. Hearing this from people you love and respect can be more than difficult to handle. It may even cause you to relapse in your healing process.

Hearing of such abuse may cause a split among family members. Finger pointing and blame, rather than accountability, becomes the norm, because when trauma occurs in the family many need a person to blame. This may cause you and others of your family to feel shame concerning the trauma of your sexual abuse. There is no way of fully knowing the effects that will result from revealing the nature of your sexual abuse at the hands of a family member until you make the decision to finally speak your truth. However, to help you understand how trauma can have a detrimental impact and strain family relationships, we will explore the evolution of the superhero Aquaman, his family, and their relationship before, during, and after the trauma that led to their eventual split.

When Aquaman suffers the trauma of losing his son Arthur Jr., he pushes the people he cares for the most further and further away. Rather than deal with the trauma he suffered, Aquaman works to mask his feelings, causing the split between him and his sidekick, Aqualad, and the separation between Aquaman and his wife, Mera. The strain of these family relationships leave him alone, altered physically and mentally, and estranged from the people he once called family. Survivors often have these same feelings of isolation from members of their family when the nature of their abuse is revealed to have involved another member of the family.

Aquaman: From Lighthearted to Ominous Truth and Trauma

Out of all the heroes of the early DC universe, Aquaman was by far the most centered, happy, and optimistic. His ability to communicate with sea animals and swim throughout the ocean in an orange and green wet suit gave the impression that he was the ultimate carefree surfer dude.

For most of the early years of the Aquaman comics, Arthur Curry (Aquaman) was fighting crime alone, patrolling the sea, and protecting his sea friends. Artists often depicted the superhero surfing on the back on a turtle or riding the fin of a shark with a smile, blonde hair flowing in the current, and confident in his actions. However, in *Adventure Comics #269*, Aquaman begins to develop a family of his own. Here, in "The Kid from Atlantis," readers are introduced to a young boy with the same abilities of communicating with animals in the ocean as Aquaman. However, unlike Aquaman, he is deathly afraid of all fish. Aquaman successfully helps the boy overcome his fear of fish. After doing this, the boy becomes Aqualad, and the two fight crime side by side.

In "The Wedding of Aquaman," Aquaman marries a woman known as Mera. Together they have a baby boy, who they call Arthur Jr. For a short time, the four are happy together as a family, until trauma strikes, splitting them all apart.

In *Adventure Comics #452*, "Dark Destiny, Deadly Dreams," Arthur Jr. is kidnapped by a villain known as Black Manta. Once kidnapped, the baby, who has lived in the ocean his entire life, is placed into a bubble that is slowly draining of seawater, suffocating the baby. The only way to save Arthur Jr. is if Aquaman and Aqualad fight to the death. Eventually, with help from his ocean friends, Aquaman manages to escape the hold Black Manta has over the two heroes and come close to but not actually kill his sidekick. Unfortunately, the rescue of Arthur Jr. comes too late. Before Aquaman can save his son, the boy suffocated and died. Filled with rage, Aquaman vows revenge on Black Manta, but Aqualad refuses to join him in his vendetta. Because of Aquaman's actions and attempt at killing Aqualad, he no longer trusts the hero, so he can no longer fight beside him.

Over time, rather than deal with the loss of his son, Aquaman spends all his time working as a superhero, pushing his wife further and further away until she leaves and he is left with nothing but his work. She says in a message left for the superhero after leaving him:

> We shared so much once—our thoughts as well as our love—but all that seemed to end when our son died. It's just taken me so long to accept it. Duty replaced love in your heart—duty to me, to Atlantis, even when its people deposed you, and duty to the Justice League. I know now that your duty to the League is the most important feeling in your life; that's why you remained with them during the crisis, rather than me. I could stay your wife without love if I was still someone important in your life, but if I don't have that, I have nothing. Goodbye, my love. Please don't try to follow ...

Now, after suffering the impact of devastating trauma that affected him and his family, the superhero that was once the happiest and optimistic of the DC universe became its most jaded. Smiles and joy no longer graced the covers of his comic, as more tensions rose between him and his half-brother, Orm. Instead, his expression is stern and his thoughts are rarely filled with the blind belief that everything will turn out for the better.

Throughout the years of Aquaman's existence, he progressed from optimistic loner in the 1940s, to happy family man in the fifties and sixties, before losing all sense of that happiness due to an inability to express the grief, sadness, and depression of the trauma he suffered to the friends and family he cared for the most. The loss of his family not only resulted in the changing of the superhero's personality, but the alteration of his appearance as well.

In the early forties, sixties, and part of the seventies, Aquaman remained the eternally optimistic hero, always smiling, riding the back of a sea animal, thoughtful of both the undersea world and the world above waters. However, by the mid-seventies, the smiles were replaced with a hard grimace and gritting teeth. He was also no longer the clean shaven, cropped blonde-haired hero of the deep. Following the trauma of losing his son, Aquaman grew a full beard and let his hair grow out to resemble that of a hard rocker. He even lost his right hand when it was stripped from his body by flesh-eating piranha in *Aquaman #2*, "Single Wet Female," By the 2000s, the clean-shaven hero of the deep returns, but the happy smiles and optimistic grin remained a thing of the past.

What Aquaman reveals about the nature of trauma is that it has the potential to rip a family apart. This is true of any trauma a family may suffer, including sexual abuse. What you have to know and accept as a male survivor beginning your journey of healing is that you cannot control the emotions and feelings of others. It does not matter whether they are members of your family, people you love, or complete strangers, the emotions, thoughts, and feelings of individuals are their own, and you cannot tell them how or what to feel or think. While this is true for others, it is also true for you. This means that as a child you had endure feelings of weakness at the hands of your abuser, having no way of combatting their suppression of who you are. You may have been told then, or even now, that your sexual abuse was impossible, that the best thing for you to do now as an adult is to forgive, forget, and move forward. However, as an adult, you do not have to endure their feelings of shame and the minimizing beliefs of your abuse. You can keep those people from infecting the progress of your healing by limiting or cutting communication with them. Doing this will allow you the space and time needed to go through your healing process unhindered.

Although you may have no control over the emotions and thoughts of those around you, you do have control over your own. This means not limiting your emotions and pushing the people who care for you away in the same way as Aquaman pushed away Mera.

It means getting the help you deserve and including those people closest to you on your journey if they choose to join you. To be and have a family takes work. If the family you were born into failed you as a child by allowing your sexual abuse to occur through negligence or knowingly causing you harm, it does not mean you have to do the same with the family you have created. You can do and become better, but you must get the help of a therapist and truly heal from the trauma of your sexual abuse. Learn to retain and build the optimism of the past by hoping that tomorrow will be a better day, no matter how painful the past may have been. You are a survivor. This means you are strong, but it does not mean you are invincible. Know when you are weak and lean on those closest to you until your strength returns, while doing the same for others. This is what it means to be more than a hero or a survivor. It's what it means to be a man.

Chapter Seven
Robin: Sexual Abuse and Parenting

You need me, and I will always be at your side. Because it will be hard for me to say this face to face, I want you to know that mother may have given me life, but you taught me how to live.

—Damian Wayne (*New Earth*)

How Abuse Affects Parenting

Being a male survivor of child sexual abuse does not mean you only identify as a survivor. Male survivors are also brothers, uncles, husbands, or even as fathers raising children of their own. What it does mean is that survivors view and approach these relationships with different emotions and reactions than others who have not been sexually abused as children. This is especially true when it comes to having and raising children of their own. As a survivor, you may not have had the healthy family relationships you deserved. Statistics state that in homes where sexual abuse has occurred there may also be alcohol, drug, or domestic abuse. This means having a model in which to understand what it means to have a healthy, happy, and stable household may not have been provided, leaving you unable to understand how to be a parent while possibly leading you toward repeating some of the same bad habits of your own parents. However, in some cases the opposite may just as well be true. Because you are a survivor of child sexual abuse and did not have a stable household as a child, you may know what you don't want in the family you create and how you want to parent. *The Courage to Heal* tells us that as a survivor of child sexual abuse you may:

- feel uncomfortable or frightened around children
- be uncomfortable being affectionate with children
- be confused about the line between appropriate and inappropriate touch
- have been abusive or fear that they might be
- have not adequately protected the children in your care
- be overprotective and keep your children from normal life experiences

As a survivor, you may also find it hard to:

- set clear boundaries with children
- balance your children's needs with your own
- feel close or connected to your children

To understand how child sexual abuse may affect you as a parent, there is no better superhero parent to examine than Batman and his relationship with his sidekick over the years of his existence. Each relationship with each of the boys who wore the costume over the years reveals a different facet of how trauma can affect a survivor's ability to parent.

Robin is the name of Batman's sidekick. Since Batman came into existence, there have been a number of young boys who have put on the costume of Robin to become the ward of the Dark Knight. Each Robin has had a different effect on Batman/Bruce Wayne as an adoptive and actual parent because of the trauma of losing his parents as a child.

Robin Number One, Dick Grayson: Maintaining Balance

As a male survivor of child sexual abuse, you may find it difficult to balance the needs of your children with your own. Because of the nature of your abuse and the trauma you suffered as a child, the need to have children, or feel as if you would be a good parent, may be minimized. This is because the effects of your sexual abuse and attempting to understand them throughout your life occupy most, if not all, of your time, pushing the job of being a supportive parent to the back burner. Unfortunately, this may mean your children feel abandoned and unsupported. This is why understanding the nature of your sexual abuse and beginning to heal from the effects is critical, especially if it means giving your children the stable home you may not have experienced as a child.

The ability to balance your own needs with those of your children can be seen and understood best in the relationship of Batman/Bruce Wayne and the first boy to wear the red, green, and yellow costume of Robin, Dick Grayson. Readers were introduced to Grayson in *Detective Comics #38,* "Robin, The Boy Wonder," as a member of a traveling circus performing in the highflying act, "The Flying Graysons." While performing in Gotham, the young boy tragically lost his parents in the same manner as Bruce Wayne. However, rather than being shot and murdered on the street as Bruce's parents were, Dick's parents were killed when gangsters rigged their rope to break, making it appear as an accident. After the accident occurs, Batman takes in the youth, trains him to fight crime, and adopts the boy as his son.

Dick began fighting crime as Batman's sidekick when he was a boy. As time progressed, he grew into a young man who, like all young men, yearned to move on and escape the shadow of his father to become a man of his own. For Dick, this meant becoming a member of the young crime fighting team, the Teen Titans, and venturing out on his own to become his own hero. Unfortunately, the need to grow and become a man was impossible for Batman to accept because, like many male survivors, he was unable to balance his own needs with those of his adopted son, Dick.

The clash of their personalities and understanding the need to balance the needs of others came to a head in *Nightwing #101*, "Nightwing Year One: Only Robins Have Wings." The story begins with falling snow, Robin racing along on a snowmobile, and running commentary about how the Boy Wonder was running late, why he stopped being Robin, and feelings he held toward his legal guardian and mentor, Bruce Wayne.

Dick starts by saying, "Both of us knew this was inevitable. With college. With the Teen Titans. With what little life I had of my own. With all that, I had to be late the one time when I was really needed. It was easier when I was just the junior partner. Now there aren't enough hours in the day . . . or the night. Both of us knew there would come a time when I wouldn't be there for backup. Or cut it too close . . ."

Later, while battling a villain known as Clayface (a supervillain made of clay and mud who can mold himself into any shape he chooses) and preventing him from kidnapping a baby, Batman becomes angry at Robin for being late. Robin attempts to apologize, explaining his work with the Teen Titans, but each time Batman cuts him off saying, "Save it."

Dick goes on to explain how the two of them never talk. He explains how they met and how Batman always pushed him to be better. Dick flashes back to a memory of crying over the bodies of his dead parents and Batman saying to him, "You can cry over them or you can take what you're feeling and do something better with it."

He flashes back to memories of training to become Robin, and each scene depicts Dick being told to, "Do it better."

When the story returns to the present, Dick tells Batman, "All my life I've been trying my best to impress you. To show you that you chose well when you offered me this job. That I wouldn't break under pressure. That I'd become what you wanted me to be." He goes on to say, "When I got home and saw the signal, I came running. I'm supposed to be your partner, not your errand Boy Wonder."

Batman responds by saying, "You should have been beside me from the start. And lately, you've been neither."

This dialogue between the two heroes reveals Robin's constant feelings of inadequacy and Batman's shortcomings as a mentor/parent to balance his own needs with those of his sidekick/son. For Batman, it's his needs, wants, and directives or nothing at all. It's this form of absolute thinking that led to the end of Dick Grayson as Robin number one, and the beginning of Dick's transcendence toward becoming a hero of his own known as Nightwing.

When the two return to the Batcave after defeating Clayface, Bruce tells Robin, "This is a war, Dick. Robin is my second . . . my lieutenant. Anything less than total devotion to the cause is simply wasting my time," before finally telling his sidekick, "You're fired, Dick! Get out of my cave."

Yes, this is a comic book. And, yes, the above scene is very over dramatic. However, as a male survivor of child sexual abuse, you may hold your children to the same impossible standards as Batman held Robin. You may refuse to acknowledge the needs and wants of your children and how they may outweigh your own. Learning to take notice of your emotions and the way you treat your children is pivotal toward not pushing them away. Parenting means balancing your needs with those of your children. This is not easy. It takes time, patience, therapy, and healing from the abuse you suffered. Without this healing, the children you love and care for may feel lost, alone, isolated, and as if they have no place in your life. To give them the support they need, you must become the parent they deserve.

Robin Number Two, Jason Todd: Protecting Your Children

Sometimes, as a survivor, you may feel as though you have not adequately protected the children in your care. This feeling, whether real or imaginary, may be because of an inability to set clear boundaries, fear of displaying the same abuse to your children that was shown to you, or actually being abusive to your children in the same way that you were abused. As a parent, it is your responsibility to protect your children. Failing to live up to that responsibility, or feeling as though you've failed to live up to those responsibilities, may make you feel like less of a human, causing bouts of depression and anxiety. These failures, whether perceived or real, are because of the abuse you suffered as a child and can be seen in the relationship of Batman and the second young boy to wear the costume of Robin, Jason Todd.

Jason appeared for the first time in *Batman #408*, "Did Robin Die Tonight?" when Batman returns to the neighborhood, Park Row, where he lost his parents on the anniversary of their murder. Each year on that date, Batman patrolled the neighborhood, walking the streets, frightening criminals, and when he ventured to his car he found the wheels of his Batmobile gone. What was more surprising was that the tires had been taken by a little boy, Jason. Batman follows the boy, realizes he's homeless, and takes in the youth to be the next Robin. As Jason grew older, Batman soon realized he was much different from Dick. Living alone for so long on the streets hardened him to criminals, leading him to sometimes break Batman's hero code and kill his opponent.

Unable to deal with or understand Jason sometimes left Bruce feeling as if he had let the boy down, but this feeling of failure did not fully take hold until Jason's murder in *Batman #427*, "Death in the Family: Part 2." In this issue, Jason finds his mother, Sheila Todd, but soon finds her working with the Joker. To try and help her escape, Jason reveals that he is Robin. Unfortunately, rather than accept his help, she turns him over to the Joker and watches as Jason is nearly beaten to death. However, before Batman can save Jason, the Joker sets off a bomb that kills both Jason and his mother. After his death, the thought of not protecting Jason and feeling as though he had caused the boy's death ripped Bruce apart. These thoughts of not protecting the child in his care led him to vow to never have another Robin, opening the position to be filled by Robin number three.

As a male survivor of child sexual abuse, your feelings of failure as a parent may be the same as Batman's after Jason's death. Unlike Batman, you do not fight crime, but you may feel as though you expose your children to unnecessary dangers that could lead to them being hurt. You may fear for the protection of your children, while longing to protect them from any and all dangers, because of the lack of protection you were given as a child. This could lead to setting unclear or unachievable boundaries for your children. While you may believe you are keeping your family from harm by remaining strict, isolating, and stern, you prevent them from living a full life, while pushing them away in the process. Understanding what it means to live and have a normal childhood may be foreign to you because no one provided you with a model. For you, dangers lurk around every corner and in every shadow, keeping you from loving your children for who they are and allowing them room for mistakes and growth.

Although you have the possibility of being an overprotective parent and keeping your children from normal life experiences, you have the potential to swing in the other direction and expose your children to dangers or poor living conditions you believe are acceptable. These dangers are present in the lives of you and your children because the model for parenting was not provided for you as a child when you were sexually abused. As a result, you may abuse your child emotionally, physically, or psychologically, because it is the only method of parenting you may know. Like Batman, you allow the children you are supposed to protect, like Jason Todd, experience the unhealthy effects of a dysfunctional home. Rather than taking your children out to battle criminals, you may expose them to the unhealthy effects of alcohol or drug abuse, while believing this way of living is acceptable. This method of parenting fails to protect children and continues the cycle of abuse or incest, rather than bringing it to an end. The only way to ensure you protect the children you love from the effects of your own sexual abuse is to address your own trauma and move forward to become the parent your children deserve.

Robin Number Three, Tim Drake: Fear

As a survivor of child sexual abuse, the odds are that you fear being or becoming a parent. You fear failing in ways your parents or guardian may have failed. You may believe being a good parent is impossible because of the sexual abuse you suffered as a child. You may fear touching or showing intimacy to a child because you're unsure about the difference between an appropriate and inappropriate touch. Thoughts such as:

- Did I sexually abuse my child when I gave them a hug, or changed their diaper?
- Am I not going to be able to stop myself from sexually abusing my child?
- Can I love my child and not victimize them?

Or you may fear being hurt by a child and have thoughts that may seem irrational such as, Is this child going to hurt me in the same way I was abused when I was their age?

These thoughts and millions more may cause you to feel uncomfortable or fear children. Depending on the nature of your abuse you may have a fear of hurting a child in your care, or them hurting you. This fear is rational and can be understood best by examining the relationship of Batman and Robin number three, Tim Drake.

Unlike the previous Robins, Tim was not adopted by Bruce Wayne. Tim had parents and a family all his own that he reported to each night after fighting crime with Batman. This created an entirely different understanding of the Robin character and how he interacted with the Dark Knight. What also made Tim different from Jason Todd and Dick Grayson was the fact that he never wanted to be anything more than Robin. He did not strive to move beyond the shadow of Batman. Instead, he strived to remain Batman's sidekick as long as possible, because he knew Batman needed a Robin.

After Jason Todd's death, Bruce vowed to never endanger the life of another boy seeking to be his sidekick. The only problem was that without a Robin, Batman became reckless, darker, heartless, and a hero who was lost as he searched for a code. Dick, now known as the hero Nightwing, and Alfred, his butler, both noticed a difference in the attitude of the hero. The difference was also noticed by a little boy who discovered Batman's secret.

Tim Drake followed the career of Batman from when he was a little boy. While watching news footage of Batman, Tim saw an acrobatic move performed by Robin number one that he saw performed by Dick Grayson when he was a member of the Flying Graysons in the traveling circus. Using that information, Tim was able to deduce that if Dick was Robin, than Bruce Wayne, his adoptive guardian, must be Batman. Tim kept this secret to himself for years, until he noticed there was no longer a Robin and the news coverage of Batman became bleaker as his attitude toward criminals had become darker and less human. Later, after revealing his secret to Dick, Tim convinced him that Batman needed a sidekick to remain sane. To help Batman retain his sanity, Tim took up the mantle of Robin against Batman's wishes. However, after saving the hero from being killed by Two Face, and not seeking revenge after the murder of his parents, Batman agreed to officially make Tim the new Robin.

What needs to be noted and understood is Batman's fear of endangering another child in his care. Batman/Bruce Wayne fears what it would mean to have a Robin by his side who could die while under his protection. Instead, by not having a Robin to ground him and remind him that he solved and fought crime not only with his head but also with his heart, the hero risks his own sanity and health to protect his child from being hurt by the effects of the trauma he suffered as a child.

What you have to know as a parent and a survivor is that, although you may fear having children, the stable relationships we build with them as adults ground your thoughts. The children you have in your life should put a smile on your face and remind you to live for others besides yourself. Including young people in your life may not only help them have the guidance of an adult, but it can also help you address the nature of the abuse you suffered, survived, and can heal from.

Robin Number Four, Damian Wayne: Parenting

Whether you are a survivor or not, parenting is about trial, failure, and trial again. No amount of planning can prepare you for having a child of your own that is your sole responsibility. It takes patience, understanding, admittance of failure, a willingness to persevere, love, more love, more patience, and much more love. As a parent, you will fail and not know what to do. However, you must know and accept that this has nothing to do with the sexual abuse you suffered as a child. It just has to do with being a parent, feeling stressed, lost, unrested, and unimaginably happy all at the same time.

Coming to terms with what it means to be a parent can be seen in the fourth Robin and biological son of Bruce Wayne, Damian Wayne. Throughout Damian's early childhood, Bruce had no idea of his son's existence. His mother, Talia, the daughter of Ra's al Ghul, kept his birth and existence a secret. She raised him as a warrior and member of the assassin organization The League of Shadows. It wasn't until Damian was about ten years old that Bruce learned of his son's existence and took him in. By then he had spent a decade training in the art of killing. This made teaching Damian to adhere to a code of not killing and following and taking direction by anyone he considered to not be his equal extremely difficult, taking time and patience.

As Damian trained to become the new Robin over a number of years, Bruce lost his temper, learned to trust his son, practiced patience, and developed a way to set clear boundaries while allowing the boy to grow, explore, and become his own person. He established trust through respect, patience, and love. Bruce learned these skills through the experienced shared with the previous three Robins. He was by no means perfect as a father and in his interactions with

Damian, but he developed and grew to be a parent, mentor, guide, friend, and confidant to his son.

As a survivor, this ability to allow independence while setting clear boundaries is the goal. It may seem impossible, but given enough time, trial, error, patience, and healing from your own trauma of sexual abuse, you can be the parent you wish to be and the one your children deserve.

Part Two:
VILLAINS

A villain is just a victim whose story hasn't been told.

-Chis Colfer

Chapter Eight
Am I a Villain?

In *Batman Special #1*, "The Player on the Other Side", the mirror opposite of Batman is presented to the reader. The masked identity of both heroes was born on the same night of June 26 under similar circumstances a few blocks from the other. While Bruce Wayne's parents were killed at gunpoint by the gangster, Joe Chill, the other boy's parents were killed by James Gordon as they attempted to rob a house. After seeing the two exit through a window, Gordon tells them to stop and places his hand on his gun. Rather than listen, the father fired a gun at the rookie cop. Taking a bullet to the chest, Gordon falls to the ground. As he falls, he pulls his gun and fires two shots. Both bullets find their mark and kill the mother and father as their son witnesses their death behind a trashcan.

The first three pages of the comic are split in half. On top is the story of Bruce Wayne's journey toward becoming Batman. The images portray the killing of his parents, the nurturing love of Leslie Thompkins after their death, Bruce training to better his mind and body, before concluding with the image of a bat he believes to be an omen. The bottom half of the pages tell a similar but different story. Like Bruce, the second boy watches as his parents are killed at the hand of a gun, but rather than a gangster holding the gun, it is a police officer. Following the death of his parents, rather than receive the nurturing love of a surrogate mother, the second young boy is placed in the care of the state in a juvenile correctional facility. It is there the boy received a different kind of training than Bruce, but just as deadly. The young boy learned the deadly use of guns, knives, and the effects of revenge, as he vowed to kill the man who killed his parents, Police Commissioner James Gordon.

With the portrayal of both men in their costumes, one in black and the other in maroon, the title pages of the comic state, "Bruce Wayne crusades against all crime, all injustice, as the dreaded

Batman. While his mirror-self wars against all law, all those who enforce the law, as the Wrath."

Throughout the story, scenes of the Wrath killing police officers with bullets, knives, and explosives are drawn and illustrated with grit only the eighties can produce, as the villain hunts for James Gordon. Three times, Batman saves the commissioner before placing him in a safe house. While attempting to find Gordon and stop Batman, the Wrath unravels the secret identity of Batman to be Bruce Wayne and how both were "born" on the same night twenty-five years prior. To eliminate all obstacles in his path toward revenge, the Wrath destroys the graves of Bruce's parents, places Alfred in the hospital, cuts the throat of a man who could have given information to Batman about his identity, and kidnaps the little-old-lady depiction of Leslie Thompkins.

The comic comes to an end with an epic battle between what is supposed to represent good and evil. Batman and the Wrath are equally matched. One knows the moves of the other, attempting to counter in the same way a shadow would match its master. Of course, Batman wins (because he is Batman), but the comic can offer a deeper understanding of the effects of trauma on an individual and their identification as either a survivor or victim.

On June 26 in Park Row, both Bruce Wayne and the other young boy were victimized after witnessing the traumatic event of their parents' deaths. One young boy was cared for and loved, while the other was sent to a correctional facility. One was forced to live a much harder life than the other, leading to the alternate views of how each saw themselves and their society.

After the death of his parents, Bruce took a vow to always fight injustice and help those in need of help. As an adult, he made the choice to become a hero. He did not hold everyone to blame for the tragedies of his past. Instead, he held criminals accountable for their actions by handing them over to law enforcement rather than seek revenge. He sought to cope with his past in the most positive way he knew and attempted to ensure no one went through the same tragedy he was forced to endure. The channeling of his actions into something positive rather than negative identifies more with the traits of a survivor than a victim.

The actions of the Wrath were just the opposite. Rather than help others in the same way as Batman, the Wrath only sought to cope with his pain, selfishly through revenge. All other individuals were viewed as either disposable pawns or obstacles to be conquered. Rather than view his actions as wrong, he viewed them as justifiable because of the abuse he suffered as a child. The channeling of his actions into something negative rather than positive identifies more with the traits of a victim rather than a survivor.

Although one young boy came to view himself as a hero and the other a villain, both were given similar opportunities to become neither a hero nor a villain, but at different times in their lives. As a child, Bruce Wayne has something the second young boy does not. He has the care, love, and affection of his adopted mother, Leslie Thompkins, and butler/father figure, Alfred Pennyworth. The second young boy only has himself. However, as an adult, the Wrath has something Batman does not. He has the love and affection of a woman. Throughout *Batman Special #1*, she begs the Wrath to walk away from his obsession for revenge and leave Gotham with her. She loves the Wrath for all his flaws, in the same way Leslie and Alfred loved Bruce. In the end, neither agreed to the request of their loved ones to heal from their trauma. Instead, Bruce Wayne became the hypervigilance hero to cope with the tragedy of losing his parents, and the Wrath continued to seek revenge to cope with his victimization. Neither chose to heal. Instead, both chose to hurt the ones who love them through their actions.

Neither Batman nor the Wrath, hero or villain, are completely correct in the strategies they use to cope with their abuse; they offer an understanding of the difference between becoming a survivor and remaining a victim. Many heroes and their actions can be identified with those of survivors, because they have a tendency to use the tragedies of their past to better themselves and sometimes others. For example, Superman lost his entire planet and parents as a child, but he chose to help others with his super abilities rather than enslave humanity; Batman's parents were murdered, but he chose to fight against crime rather than seek revenge or remain rich and do nothing at all; the Flash's mother was murdered, but he chose to become a forensics scientist to put criminals behind bars rather than self-medicate through drugs and alcohol.

The actions of villains are different than those of heroes, and they sometimes resemble the actions of individuals who identify as victims. Rather than cope with the tragedies of the past in a positive way, victims view the world as the enemy and the source of all their problems. The coping strategies of victims are more negative, often less healthy, and can often be portrayed in the actions and beliefs of villains rather than heroes. For example, Lex Luthor denies any wrongdoing in his quest to destroy Superman, viewing himself as the hero rather than the villain; the Joker choses to cause chaos throughout the lives of others to gain a semblance of control in his life; and even heroes such as Roy "Speedy" Harper and Harvey Dent have the capacity to become villains without proper healing.

However, as a survivor of child sexual abuse, it is important to know that the world is not a comic book. There are no superheroes or evil villains. Both archetypes are flawed and wrong and, hence, why this guide is broken into three parts—heroes, villains, and healing—to recognize the flaws in the coping strategies that identify with those of villains and heroes. The only way to stop having the viewpoint of a victim is to heal.

Some habits and beliefs you have developed as a male survivor have allowed you to excel and succeed throughout life. These traits may resemble those of heroes, allowing others to view you and your actions as positive. However, over time, they can lead to an unhealthy way of living, and that is why striving to reach heroism should not be your goal. Unfortunately, some of the actions you took to cope with the trauma of being sexually abused as a child may fall in line with the habits and beliefs of villains rather than heroes. This section will help you to identify some of those traits and the need to seek help to overcome the trauma of your past and move beyond the realm of heroes and villains to become a complete person.

Chapter Nine
Lex Luthor: Denial

I can't think of a morning I haven't woken up with the thought of strangling you. That sanctimonious image of yours fooled everyone except me. Because I know evil.

—Lex Luthor. *Superman/Batman: Public Enemies* (2008)

Lex Luthor and Male Survivor's Denial of Their Abuse

As a male survivor of child sexual abuse, you have learned to cope with the abuse you suffered. Coping may have meant working to the point of no longer acknowledging the trauma you suffered, or becoming an overachiever in school, work, and life. One of the major coping strategies you may have utilized as a child, and now as an adult, is denial that you were ever sexually abused. It may also involve denying that the sexual abuse you suffered as a child affected your life in any way, blaming others for many problems in your life, whether that be your abuser or any other person who challenges your thoughts or beliefs. Continued denial of the abuse you suffered can become an infection that seeps into all parts of your life. If left untreated, it can cause you to no longer consider yourself a survivor, but react and interact with others as a victim who is only capable of being constantly abused and mistreated throughout all aspects of their life. Possible reasons for this denial may be to:

- protect yourself from remembering traumatic events of your past
- allow respite from the knowledge that you were a child with no power to protect yourself
- give you the mental well-being to work
- make it more bearable to face a reality where you weren't sexually abused

One possible explanation for denying sexual abuse as a man is because many men are under the belief that mental illness and trauma are not real medical conditions, but moral decisions. This belief in mental illness and the negative effects of the sexual abuse you may have suffered as a child is the primary reason only 9 percent of men receive counseling or therapy after suffering a traumatic experience. The same is true for boys from ages nine through seventeen who suffer from depression, versus girls of the same age.

For these statistics to change and eliminate denial that men cannot be sexually abused as children, there must no longer be a separation between physical and spiritual health. All individuals, whether male or female, must view themselves as whole beings with access to good, affordable mental health services. There must also be strong male role models to set the example for boys who share the same cultural and ethnic background. Doing this will allow young men to observe and know that it is okay to get help, and it will ensure current and future generations no longer have a negative stigma toward getting help for poor mental health after experiencing trauma and abuse. Creating these connections between men and boys will increase mental health as well as lower rates of homicide, suicide, and alcohol and drug abuse, according to Project Cornerstone in 2009.

To understand how denial can have a negative effect on your life and your view of yourself as a survivor of child sexual abuse, there is no better example than Superman's archenemy, Lex Luthor.

Lex Luthor is the archenemy of Superman. Although he has no superpowers, he is extremely intelligent. Unlike Superman, Luthor is human. Also unlike Superman, Lex uses his genius selfishly to kill his enemy, to the detriment of humanity. Although Lex is often portrayed as the villain of the story, he often views himself as the hero, ridding humanity of the menace, Superman. In the same way survivors may deny the negative effects the abuse they suffered in the past is having on their lives, Lex often denies any of his actions were in any way wrong. Instead, he portrays himself as the victim and Superman as his abuser.

Friends Become Enemies

It has often been the case that heroes and their archenemies were friends before they became enemies. Superman and Lex Luthor are no different. In fact, the origins of their friendship were explored in *Adventure Comics #271*, "How Luthor Met Superboy," when Superboy and a young Lex Luthor meet for the first time as boys.

In this comic, Lex saves Superboy from a kryptonite meteorite that fell from space and threatened to kill the pint-sized hero. Lex uses his tractor to push the rock into the water, saving the young superhero. To repay Lex for saving his life, Superboy builds Lex a new laboratory filled with rare chemicals at super speed. Later in the story, Lex works with the chemicals, but while attempting to create a kryptonite antidote to thank Superboy for the laboratory, Lex accidentally starts a chemical fire. He calls for help, and when Superboy arrives he blows out the flames. However, rather than thank Superboy for saving his life, Lex blames him for destroying the antidote and the gas fumes that caused him to go bald. Superboy apologizes, but from that moment on, Lex blames Superboy for all his problems and shortcomings as a scientist, while denying any of his own wrongdoing. You, as a male survivor of child sexual abuse, may suffer the same denial about the trauma of your abuse and its effects on the actions you take and the interactions you have with others.

In actuality, both Superboy and Lex were at fault. It was because of Superboy's rash actions to blow out the fire rather than enter to save Lex that the kryptonite antidote was destroyed. However, it was because of Lex's clumsiness that the fire began, causing him to go bald as a reaction to the fumes of the chemicals. The difference between the hero and the villain is that Superboy recognized his role in the problem and apologized. Unfortunately, Lex cannot do the same and blames Superboy for all his problems.

As a male survivor of child sexual abuse, you may behave, react, and think in the same way as Lex, blaming others for all your life's problems. It is true you were sexually abused as a child, but in no way was that your fault. You were a child who had little to no power over your abuser. However, as an adult you have more control over your life and power in the actions you take than you did as a child. Then you were powerless. Now, as an adult, you have more control and can decide to begin to heal from the traumas of your past and how they alter your thinking and actions. Unlike Lex, you can recognize the mutual faults your actions and thinking had to cause problems along with the thoughts and actions of others.

What you must understand is that no one is perfect. This is not an excuse to excuse your abuser from the sexual trauma you suffered at their hands. This is meant to help you understand that the constant denial of the sexual abuse you suffered and an understanding of the negative effects it has caused on the way you think may lead to a view of yourself as *being* perfect, a view of always being in the right, or the victim, or attacked. As adults, being a survivor means knowing you were weak then, accepting there was nothing you could do in the past, but having the strength now to take control of your life, heal, and be the person you always wished to be.

Will this be difficult? Absolutely. Will the denial you have and the success you make have set backs? Definitely. However, today, you are alive, breathing, and surviving the horrific trauma of your sexual abuse. This means you are strong and can heal from your past. All it takes is time, effort, and willingness to believe in yourself, while not denying the truth of your past. Unfortunately, with constant denial of your sexual abuse, the happiness you sought and developed for yourself can be destroyed by your own hands in the same way Luthor destroyed his own happiness seeking revenge and denying his own wrongdoing.

The End of the World

In 1963, Superman and Lex Luthor had a fistfight on an alien planet with a red sun to determine the all-time victor in *Superman #164*, "The Showdown Between Luthor and Superman." The deal between the two was that if Luthor won, Superman would be left on the planet and not be allowed to return to Earth. If Superman won, Lex would return to prison to finish his sentence without attempting to escape. As the story progresses, the two fight but become separated during a dust storm. In part two of the comic, Lex befriends the local inhabitants of the planet and uses his scientific knowledge to rebuild machines and robots developed by the inhabitant's ancestors. By the time Superman finds Lex, who promises to find more water and reestablish the technology left by their ancestors, praise Luthor as the savior of their planet.

When Superman and Lex continue their fight, the inhabitants cheer for Luthor as the hero and Superman as the villain. However, the story ends with Lex throwing the fight and leaving with Superman to return to Earth, but not before asking Superman to stop at an icy planet to hurl large glaciers of ice to the alien world in order to replenish the water supply. The people praised Luthor for keeping his promise and erected a statue in his honor.

Over the years, Lex returned to the planet many times, and the people praised him as their leader. By the 1983 *Action Comics #544*, "Luthor Unleashed," Lex had changed the alien planet from a rural civilization into a scientific marvel the inhabitants now called Lexor. Lex even married a woman who gave him a son. When Luthor arrives on the planet in the comic battered and barely conscious after being defeated by Superman (again), he saw his son for the first time and vowed to become a new man. He tells his wife, Adora, that he is now "a man who will stay where he belongs, here with the family he has always secretly longed for! My life as a criminal on Earth . . . the never-ending hate-war I've always waged against Superman. All of it seems a pathetic wasted life now! I can't erase my sordid past, but I can put it behind me!"

Unfortunately, no matter how hard Lex tries, he cannot stop the hatred he feels for Superman, so much so that he developed a super suit that could destroy Superman if and when he ever arrived on Lexor to take Luthor back to Earth to answer for his crimes. The only problem was that Lex tested the suit by destroying cities and buildings on his own planet in disguise, causing fear and confusion on an already peaceful world. This means that when Superman arrived to take Lex back to Earth, and Luthor fought Superman in the super suit he had created, the people saw the evil, armored Lexurian who had been destroying their homes was none other than Lex Luthor himself. It was then that they saw Lex as the villain and not the hero.

The story ends tragically with the destruction of Lexor. Lex shoots a beam of energy that deflects off of Superman and hits an earthquake rod that travels to the core of the planet, setting off a chain reaction that destroys the planet and all its people, including Lex's wife and son. Superman survives (of course), and as he flies away he thinks to himself, "I always suspected Luthor might become the victim of his own evil one day! But I never dreamed he would blast an entire race into oblivion along with him!"

However, Lex did not die. Instead, the reader sees him, clad in his super suit, rise over the edge of the crater with tears in his eyes. Rather than take responsibility for any of his actions and the trauma he inflicted on himself and others, he continued to deny his role as a villain. On the last page he thinks to himself, "You've taken my family from me. You've taken my world from me. Until now, I always thought I hated you as much as any one being could hate another! But I was wrong. Until today, I didn't even know the meaning of the word! I'm coming for you Superman, and I have only begun to hate!"

What Lex helps to illustrate for survivors is that denying your abuse long enough can tear apart the world you have built to protect yourself from the trauma of your past, in the same way Luthor's constant denial of his role as a villain tore the happiness he had established from its core. As a male survivor of child sexual abuse, you are not a villain. You were victimized, but you are not a victim. You are a survivor. Denying your abuse means denying your strength and allowing it to continue to be controlled by your abuser. You are stronger and more capable than you may believe. You can and deserve to heal. Everyone does.

Chapter Ten

The Synaptic Kid and The Joker: Hypervigilance, Chaos, and Sanity

Madness is the emergency exit. You can just step outside, and close the door on all those dreadful things that happened. You can lock them away ... forever.

-The Joker, *Batman* "The Killing Joke"

Batman and The Joker Struggle for Control Through Hypervigilance and Chaos

Maintaining control is a large part of what it means to cope with the sexual abuse you suffered as a child. For most individuals, maintaining this control means being hypervigilant and needing to maintain a tight control over all aspects of your life, and often even the lives of those around you. This may mean always placing your keys or shoes in the same location, controlling the flow of a conversation to ensure it never drifts into topics you know nothing about, never entering a room without knowing or having access to the exits, refusing to attempt anything new because of lack of knowledge, and control over every nuance of the expedition. It also may mean planning for every outcome, in an attempt to never again lose the power that was taken from you when you were sexually abused as a child.

While hypervigilance ensures maintaining power through constant monitoring and planning, creating chaos means maintaining control by taking the power of others to monitor and plan for the future. This method is effective because some survivors live most comfortably when they are fixing a problem rather than planning for one. Without this ever-present chaos, the idea of a normal day and life is terrifying.

Both types of survivors, whether hypervigilant or creators of chaos, are often defined by the actions they take to maintain control over their lives and keep a semblance of power. These survivors, without access to either hypervigilance or chaos, lose an understanding of who they are, the abuse they suffered, and their own identity. This is why the need for therapy and healing is of critical importance. Without proper help to understand the behaviors that may dictate the life of a survivor, it can lead to a harmful lifestyle where feelings of insanity, sadness, and depression run amuck as they attempt to live and build normal lives. In a way, attempting to build a stable life without first addressing the unstable foundation of childhood sexual abuse will lead to the eventual sabotage of happiness, control, and power originally sought.

To help understand how a refusal to address tendencies of either hypervigilance or creating chaos may lead to sadness, being trapped, and insanity, there is no better example than the hero, Batman, and the villain, the Joker. Bruce Wayne lost his parents when they were murdered when he was a boy. When this occurred, he lost control of his life and felt powerless. To regain the power that was taken when his parents were murdered, and to ensure he always remained in control, Bruce became hypervigilant by training, learning, and planning for all situations to combat crime and become Batman. Survivors of sexual abuse may also feel this need to become hypervigilant throughout their lives to regain some control and power that was taken when they were sexually abused. Without this, survivors feel lost and are unable to cope with their abuse without getting help and healing.

The Joker is the archenemy of Batman. While Batman may be hypervigilant in all parts of his life, the Joker not only survives, but thrives on chaos. Rather than planning for life's difficulties and challenges, he gains control and power over others through the disruption of order. His chaos knocks others off center, giving him the upper hand, because disorder is how he functions best. Survivors who thrive in chaotic circumstances behave in the same way as the Joker. And, like the Joker, when life is no longer chaotic, they feel out of control, with no power over their lives.

Insane in Sanity: Hypervigilance

In *Detective Comics #633*, "Identity Crisis," Bruce Wayne is forced to live a life without Batman as his secret identity and goes crazy in the process—sort of.

The story begins with Bruce dressed in a two-thousand-dollar evening suit emerging from the Gotham River with no memory of how he got there or why. Unable to remember anything, he hails a cab and makes his way home, hoping Alfred can give him some answers. Instead, when he enters, dripping water all over the floor, and asks Alfred what cases or unfinished business he was attending to the night before, Alfred replies that he wasn't working on anything and that he has a reputation to think of. Alfred continues by telling Bruce to get out his wet clothes before he catches double pneumonia. Confused, he takes a hot shower, hoping it will jog his memory, but it doesn't.

After the shower, Bruce makes his way to the Batcave, using the secret entrance behind a bookshelf in his study. The only problem is the entrance is not there. Shocked and frightened, he calls Alfred, thinking maybe he changed the system to update security measures. Instead, the butler tells his master he has no idea what he's talking about. The hypervigilance and need for constant control, understanding, and hold of power causes Bruce to panic. Fighting to stay calm, he asks Alfred to give him access to the basement so he can investigate what he was doing last night to make him end up in the river. Alfred obeys and leads Bruce to the basement, where he opens the door and finds nothing but pipes, boxes, and chests. Bruce panics, runs down the steps, and searches his mind for a possible explanation. Instead, he remains hypervigilant and grasps for control.

Bruce returns upstairs and demands to know what has happened to the Batcave, but Alfred has no idea what he is speaking of, mentions how he doesn't understand how anything dealing with

Batman has to do with him, and leaves to polish some brass. Bruce sits, confused and lost, when Tim Drake, Bruce's adopted son, enters. Relieved and frantic to see the boy he knew as Robin, he tells the boy to hit him, in an attempt to wake up from the nightmare. Tim uppercuts Bruce across the chin, but nothing changes. Instead, he becomes frightened and confused about why Bruce believes he is Batman, Wayne Manor has a Batcave, and he is Robin. In a panic, Tim goes to get help from Alfred.

When Alfred enters, Bruce tells the butler that he is Batman. Alfred thinks Bruce is being ridiculous. To prove Bruce is not Batman, Alfred turns on the television to reveal Batman on the news attempting to save a woman and child from a hostage situation. Bruce panics further, losing all semblance of control, and decides to take back the only power he can by revealing the Batman on the news as an imposter. He has no Batsuit or Batmobile, but instead takes a ski mask and his car. Before arriving at the hostage scene, Bruce stops at a sporting goods store and buys mountain climbing equipment. From there he makes his way to the hostage situation, puts on the ski mask, climbs the adjacent building, and makes his way inside.

Once in, Bruce sees Batman in action. Both take down the criminals, but when the hostages are safe, Bruce attacks Batman, calling him an impostor. His plan was to defeat Batman quickly, but Bruce is defeated instead. Before he can be taken into custody, Bruce hits Batman across the head with his mountain climbing equipment and runs away, as the police shoot to kill. Bruce makes it to his car and back home, unsure of everything and feeling as if he has no control over his life.

Standing in the basement of Wayne Manor, Bruce attempts to make sense of how the entire Batcave was moved and disappeared, when he sees the corner of the Batcave computer hidden behind a stonewall. He hurries to bring Alfred into the basement when, for only a moment, Alfred's legs are replaced by wheels. More confused than ever, the doorbell rings. Bruce answers the door to find Batman. He punches Bruce to the ground, removes his cowl, and reveals the face of Bruce Wayne. Both look at the other and panic spreads as the Bruce on the floor transforms into a grotesque kid with a bulging, bubbling head. Batman tells the boy he's not Bruce Wayne but an upstart psychic called the Synaptic Kid. The illusion drops as the boy screams when he sees his true form in the mirror.

The comic ends with the Synaptic Kid in a hospital bed, unable to move or speak, as Batman stands over the bed of the psychic who tried to read his mind to find out his secret identity and went crazy in the process. Although the comic revealed that Bruce Wayne was an impostor being controlled by the Synaptic Kid, it reveals a lot about the need for survivors to maintain control through hypervigilance, and what happens when the power of control is taken away without proper understanding and healing. For survivors, losing the power to have control over every part of their life is like losing their mind. Being hypervigilant has become a coping strategy for so long that it has also become a part of their identity. Without proper understanding of a survivor's need for control to regain some sense of the power taken from them when they were sexually abused, the sharing of that control with others may never take place and it could lead to the destruction of the world they have built.

While hypervigilance is one side of the survivors need for control, the other is creating and causing chaos. When a survivor lacks the ability to cause chaos or participate in a chaotic situation, the effects can be the same as Batman losing his ability to become hypervigilant. The survivor's world that was built on unsteady ground begins to topple , until they are re-exposed to the chaos or properly heal.

There is no better example of chaos and its effects than the Joker and what happens when he no longer allows himself to be the Joker.

Insane in Sanity: Chaos

In *Batman: Legends of the Dark Knight #66*, "Going Sane," the comic begins with a news report and Police Commissioner Gordon watching, as there has been no sign of the Joker or Batman for weeks after the Joker was stopped in an attempt to kidnap a councilwoman. The scene cuts to Alfred alone in the Batcave, worried and alone, before continuing with the nightmares of a man with a long chin. He dreamed of a grotesque bat and the face of the Joker. Commentary around the pictures explain the man's internal battle with his demons as he attempts to stay sane. He thinks, as a monstrous bat swoops down from the sky:

> *The monster. Black wings. Dead eyes. After me. Always after me. Trying to push me down. Into the river. Drown me. Gotta run and hide, change my name, change my face so he'll never find me! My face? That's not my face! That's the monster! The real monster! Pasty-white skin! Awful soulless grin! He hates me! More than the bat does. He's hungry for me! Wants to cut up my life, slice it to ribbons, kill all that's decent and good in me and make me like him! Stop it! Stop laughing at me! Why won't you leave me alone, both of you? I hate you! Batwings, clown-face, push me down! Cutting me up . . . can't stay afloat . . . can't catch my breath! Oh, God, it hurts! Oh, God, I'm drowning!*

Although this dialogue is fictional, it may sound familiar to the internal dialogue you've had with yourself in order to remain sane and prevent yourself from causing or participate in making chaos. Like the man suffering from the nightmare in the above passage, you may feel the world you have built is a dream waiting to fall apart, and it's all you can do to keep from going crazy.

The comic continues with the man waking from his nightmare to a news report on the television that explains the disappearance of Batman and the Joker. The man gets ready for work, counting his blessings for moving to Gotham, having some money in the bank from an inheritance, and a job as an accountant. As he walks down the hall of his apartment building, he thinks how his life would be complete if he had a girl in his life, when he runs into a woman in the hall (literally) and knocks her groceries to the floor. He picks them up, carries them to the woman's apartment, and the two begin a relationship. She says her name is Rebecca and his is Joseph Kerr.

Joseph's nightmares became more vivid and terrifying as he struggles to block the images of the monstrous bat and the menacing clown. As he dreams, he battles with himself, before waking up screaming. *The dream. Again. But worse this time. Why does it scare me so? Makes me feel like the whole world's closing in on me, like there's someone inside of me with a knife trying to hack his way out.*

The appeal of this comic, as a survivor of child sexual abuse, is how it not only highlights the effects of ignorance, denial, and attempts to ignore trauma and mental health not only affects the lives of survivors, but the lives of people closest to them as well. Throughout the comic, illustrator Joe Staton does an amazing job portraying the sadness and internal struggle of Joseph as he fights to contain the chaos of the Joker, but writer J. M. DeMatteis truly captures the worry, anxiety, and fear of a partner watching the person they love struggle through mental illness.

Rebecca explains this worry and fear best through the internal dialogue that accompanies the graphics. She states and explains:

> *I could feel his terror, his confusion, radiating off him in waves. But the funny thing is it only made me love him more. Love? Love is too small a word for what I felt. I wasn't exactly the kind if woman who'd had lots of men in her life. And he was wonderful. Gentle. Kind. Thoughtful. He'd buy me flowers, bring me chocolates, for no reason at all. He was a jewel, my Joseph was. A treasure. But I knew even as he struggled to deny it that there was something wrong. Some secret pain, some hidden sorrow that just wouldn't let him go. That night, when he got so angry, when he almost hit me, I shouldn't have let him go. I should have gone after him, followed him into the elevator, made him come with me to see a psychiatrist right then and there. Why didn't I? I guess deep down I was afraid that if I took Joseph to a doctor, if we found out what was really troubling him, he'd change and I'd lose the only man who ever loved me. Funny thing is, in the end I lost him anyway.*

What's amazing is that the reader begins to root for Joseph, wanting him to win. The reader wants him to get rid of the demons he carries in the form of Batman and the Joker to have a happily-ever-after with Rebecca. The only problem is that trauma and mental illness are not switches that can be flipped either on or off at will. The chaos Joseph yearns to have throughout his life can only truly go away with help and battling the demons in the dark, rather than running and hiding from them.

As a male survivor of child sexual abuse, you may suffer from post-traumatic stress disorder (PTSD) that requires either hypervigilance or consistent battles to accept the norms of reality rather than the nightmares of the past. To overcome it, you must receive help from experienced professionals who are trained to help survivors heal from the effects of their childhood sexual abuse, without which, sanity and normalcy are an impossibility.

Neither hypervigilance or chaos, hero or villain, Batman or Joker are who you should seek to become. Rather, you should fight to be the best version of yourself by defeating the traumas of your past sexual abuse through proper healing and understanding to create a durable, manageable, and lasting future.

Chapter Eleven
Two-Face: The Dissociated Man

Dissociation and Identity

Sometimes the person we wish to be is not who we become. Unlike the superhero Captain Marvel discussed previously in the section on heroes, sometimes dissociation can cause a split of identities that do more harm than good. This dissociation can result from an attempt to repress and deny the trauma of child sexual abuse while overcoming negative stigmas. The internal battle you may fight as a survivor of child sexual abuse to repress the trauma of your past and attempt to play the role of being "normal" or a "real man" may tear you apart from the inside out, leaving you lost and struggling to maintain the life you created for yourself and your family.

Unfortunately, this was the fate of Harvey Dent, a hero who turned into the villain Two-Face. After having acid thrown on his face, District Attorney Harvey Dent becomes Two-Face, unable to differentiate between good and evil without the flip of a silver dollar. The trauma of his childhood abuse and the damage done to his face split his personality. Past and present trauma of survivors may cause them to dissociate in the same way as Harvey, creating different personalities to cope with the trauma of their past, wishing to become the hero, but becoming the villain instead.

As discussed previously, if a survivor dissociates from their body they:

may not feel pleasure in physical activities

aren't aware of messages their bodies give them

feel numb or disconnected from physical sensations

111

are often on high alert for danger

are unable to relax or feel physically safe

Although this is true of individuals who suffer from dissociation, when children are unable to physically escape pain, terror, and despair of severe abuse, they sometimes create new selves when diagnosed with dissociative identity disorder (DID). These identities allow the child to survive, and while they may be bothersome as an adult, the way to heal from them is by addressing the trauma that caused DID to become a necessity in the first place. This means addressing childhood sexual abuse, rather than denying and attempting to mask its effects of that it even happened. The Batman character Harvey Dent will help understand this disorder and the need to heal from past trauma, rather than believing you must heal or join the dissociated identities as he fights for control.

Becoming the Villain

In the 1990 *Batman Annual #14,* "The Eye of the Beholder," readers are given the origins of the villain Two-Face and how he began as a hero. The story begins with the flipping of a coin, darkness, and a nightmare. Harvey Dent sits up in bed in a cold sweat, as his wife holds him, calming him down. Harvey reaches to the nightstand and picks up a two-headed silver dollar recently given to him by his father.

The story cuts from Harvey and continues with a psychopathic killing doctor who murders senior citizens with surgical equipment. Although the killer confesses to Batman, he is unable to testify because he's ... well ... a man dressed as a bat who fights crime as a vigilante, and he would not be allowed to take the stand as a character witness. However, without Batman's testimony, Harvey attempts to convict the killer as best he can. Unfortunately, the killer passes a polygraph test and is found not guilty.

After being found innocent, the killer doctor tells Harvey he was able to pass the polygraph because he has two separate personalities; one is an upstanding member of the medical community, and the other a killer who comes out when he is able to get away with murder. He confesses to Harvey because he has already been found innocent, and he senses that Harvey is the same as himself.

Before leaving Harvey kneeling on the floor, clutching his silver dollar, panicking, and in a cold sweat, he tells Harvey, "Let it go. Give it free rein. But only at the proper time. And the proper place. All you need to remember is one simple rule. Never mix business with pleasure." It's at that moment that Two-Face begins to take shape.

Later that night, Harvey calls the doctor and tells him, "I've taken your advice," as the doctor's house explodes.

As the story continues, Harvey holds a secret conversation with Batman and Jim Gordon, the police commissioner, on the roof of the police station. There, Harvey asks Batman to help gather evidence on the city's criminals to use in court. Batman agrees.

For a while, the two are successful in putting away criminals, until Harvey asks Batman to kill a suspect and plant evidence to prove their guilt. Of course, Batman refused and grew concerned over Harvey's mental state. Dent only got worse. Nightmares of his father flipping the coin and Harvey stating that he was a good boy, beating a person nearly to death after being attacked, and daydreams of shooting people in the courtroom became uncontrollable dissociations. However, Harvey did not become truly lost until crime boss Vincent Maroni took the stand and threw acid in Harvey's face in an attempt to kill him. Instead, it left one side of Harvey's face horribly scarred and allowed the villain Two-Face to be born.

After the accident, Harvey sits on his bed in the hospital flipping the two-sided silver dollar that was now scorched by acid on one side, while thinking to himself, *I'm a good boy. Good boys don't do bad things. Bad boys don't do good things! All my life, I tried to do good. All my life I kept down the bad. The bad stayed inside me, small and ugly, but hidden. No more. Now I can't hide it. Now I'm marked like a card. Or a coin.*

As a male survivor, you may have had the same thoughts as Harvey Dent, even if you have not been diagnosed with DID. You may believe that you're tainted and will never be good. You may believe the sexual abuse was your fault, that there is no way to be redeemed for a mistake you may have made in your past, or that any good you have done cannot make up for your past. This is absolute thinking—black or white, right or wrong, good or evil views of the world that lead to a belief in there being only heroes or villains.

Harvey's view of himself, his actions, and the actions of others is wrong. There is middle ground. No one is either sinner or saint, and no one is perfect. Coming to terms with this truth and truly believing there was nothing you could have possibly done to warrant sexual abuse as a child is the only way to heal from DID, the traumatic thoughts of your sexual abuse, and beginning to view yourself as a whole individual who is capable of love. Unfortunately, this is a lesson Harvey never learned.

After killing the man who gave Maroni the acid that scarred his face, Harvey went to his father's hotel and attempted to kill him as well. Although unsuccessful, it was revealed by the end of the story that Harvey's father was an alcoholic and gambler who used to beat Harvey after making him bet tails on a two-sided half dollar. This caused Harvey to develop an evil second identity that became repressed as he studied law. The second identity did not resurface until years later when his father gave him the silver dollar.

Memories have a way of staying repressed until they are triggered by events in the present, or the mind feels that the body is in a safe place to handle the trauma of the past. Rarely do individuals feel prepared to heal from traumatic abuse, but it is a journey survivors have to choose to participate in to become healthy, whole individuals. It takes work, commitment, regression, and steps forward. Healing does not happen overnight. However, the fact that you survived the sexual abuse of your past it evidence of strength you may not believe you have. You can do more, accomplish more, and be more than you ever believed possible. All it takes is a willingness to forgive yourself and the conscious decision to heal.

Chapter Twelve
Green Lantern, Speedy, and Mister Zsasz: Addiction and Self-Harm

This. This is what I am. This is who I am. Come hell or high water, if I deny it I deny everything I've ever done. Everything I've ever fought for.

—Green Arrow, *Green Arrow Vol. 2 #51*

They gave me a home and family and friendship. They made me want to be a better man. And not they've given me the greatest gift of all. No matter how impossible the odds, they'll face it like heroes.

—Roy "Speedy" Harper

We're robots, Doctor Temple. Zombies driven by the desires of the flesh and the fears of the psyche. There is no free will.

—Mister Zsasz, *The Batman Chronicles #3*

Addiction and Self-Harm

In 1998, the Center for Disease Control and Kaiser Health Plan's Department of Prevention Medicine conducted an experiment called the Adverse Childhood Experiences (ACE) Study. The ACE study involved the cooperation of over 17,000 middle-aged, middle-class Americans who agreed to help researchers study Americans study nine categories of childhood abuse and household dysfunction:

- Recurrent physical abuse
- Recurrent emotional abuse
- Contact sexual abuse
- An alcohol and / or drug abuser in the household

- An incarcerated household member
- A household member who is chronically depressed, mentally ill, institutionalized, or suicidal
- Mother is treated violently
- One or no parents
- Emotional or physical neglect

The study found that as the number of ACEs increased, the risk for health problems increased as well. Health problems such as:

- Alcoholism and alcohol abuse
- Chronic obstructive pulmonary disease (COPD)
- Depression
- Fetal death
- Health-related quality of life
- Illicit drug use
- Ischemic heart disease (IHD)
- Liver disease
- Risk for intimate partner violence
- Multiple sexual partners
- Sexually transmitted diseases (STDs)
- Smoking
- Suicide attempts
- Unintended pregnancies
- Early initiation of smoking
- Early initiation of sexual activity
- Adolescent pregnancy

These health problems reveal that ACEs have a strong impact on adolescent health, substance abuse, sexual behavior, the risk of re-victimization, and stability of relationships. It also means that the higher the ACE score, the greater risk of heart disease, liver disease, HIV, STDs, and other risks for the leading causes of death. Individuals with six or more ACEs that were compared to individuals with one or no ACEs were found to have a reduction to the longevity of their life by twenty years.

As a male survivor of child sexual abuse, you may qualify for many ACEs found during this study. Unfortunately, this means your life is more at risk than those who came from a stable household with one or no ACEs. What this study truly reveals is that in an attempt to cope with the abuse and trauma of your childhood, you may have become addicted to drugs, alcohol, sex, harmed yourself through self-inflicted wounds, or attempted suicide to relieve the pain caused by the abuse of your past.

Many survivors, at one point or another, turn to addiction and self-harm to cope with the effects of their sexual abuse, because it means they have the ability to numb the internal pain they may be feeling, while also making them feel alive and happy. Unfortunately, addictions and self-harm can affect your health or even cause death. These addictions are common because, although sexual abuse may have been present in the home, they also may have included alcohol abuse, drug abuse, or domestic violence. These addictions do not make you a bad person in any way, but they can lead to habitual behaviors that are reminiscent of the villains in comics and victims in reality. These behaviors require the help and guidance of professionals in organizations such as Alcoholics Anonymous (AA), therapy, and group counseling. This is not because individuals who have developed an addiction are not strong, but because getting the help and support of those who have lived through the same trauma provides a new sense of help and support needed when the pain of the past becomes too overwhelming. It is a primary reason for the publication of this book, to allow male survivors the strength to heal by knowing they are not alone in their abuse.

To understand how addiction and self-harm can and do affect all individuals, whether they are rich, poor, or viewed by others or themselves as a hero or villain, the addiction of drugs and their effects will be explored using the hero Green Arrow and his sidekick, Roy "Speedy" Harper, to show that even heroes can sometimes stray.

Self-harm will be explored using the villain Mister Zsasz and his view of humanity.

Addictions: Their Causes and Effects

In 1971, Green Lantern and Green Arrow teamed up for a series of thirteen comics that addressed social issues of the time period. One of those issues was drug addiction, which was discussed in the DC comics "Snowbirds Don't Fly" and "They Say It'll Kill Me. But They Won't Say When" in *Green Lantern/Green Arrow #85-86*, when Green Arrow's sidekick, Roy "Speedy" Harper became addicted to heroin when trying to overcome feelings of loneliness and sadness. The comics received national attention, awards, and a letter of commendation from New York City Mayor John Lindsay.

The story begins when Oliver Queen, also known as Green Arrow, is attacked and shot with an arrow from a crossbow by three teenagers attempting to mug him. After being released from the hospital and calling the Green Lantern, AKA Hal Jordan, for help because his arm is in a sling, Oliver inspects the arrow and realizes it's one of his own. Although he admits leaving numerous arrows at crime scenes, he expresses worry to Green Lantern that he had not heard from his sidekick, Speedy, in over a month. The two make their way to an abandoned building to get to the bottom of where the muggers got his arrow and then to find Speedy.

The two enter the building and find one of Green Arrow's muggers banging on a door in the basement, begging for a fix. After taking the dealer into custody and getting the kid to the hospital, they get information about where to find the other two muggers. The two heroes drop in on two kids, one Chinese and one black, as they talk about the reason why doing drugs makes life more bearable after being called a "chink" or a "nigger" all day. When Arrow sees Roy hiding in the shadows with the two addicts, he tells the sidekick he isn't surprised to see him. He explains how he figured when Roy went missing he was actually investigating the narcotics ring as an undercover agent. Roy played along as Arrow and Lantern took the two muggers/addicts to the whereabouts of their primary distributor. Arrow told Roy to stay behind because he looked pale.

While in transport, Arrow begins to roughhouse and talk down to the addicts. Lantern tells Arrow not to be so rough on the kids. Instead of easing off, Arrow says, "Oh, buzz off, Lantern! Look, sure I'm ticked off at the pushers because they prey on weaknesses, but that doesn't mean my heart bleeds for junkies! Life is tough for everyone! If you want to claim humanity, you don't crawl into a drugged stupor!"

Arrow's attitude toward people addicted to drugs is the same held by many people in not only the seventies, but now as well. The perpetuating belief that people need to pull themselves up by their own bootstraps is what keeps many individuals addicted to drugs and not getting the mental treatment and support they need. It is these negative stigmas and false beliefs that lead many to self-medicate and become addicted to drugs in the first place.

The comic continues with the two heroes entering an airfield hanger with the two young addicts. They all enter looking for the distributors, but the heroes are double-crossed by the kids and knocked unconscious. To get away, the dealers shoot Arrow and Lantern with heroin and call the police. When the police arrive, Roy appears and tells the officers to look for the "junkies" in a different place, as he moves Arrow and Lantern. When the two regain consciousness, the three of them escape, Arrow and Lantern attempt to deal with the effects of their hangovers, and they question why anyone would want to do drugs.

It's then that Roy attempts to explain why people may want to use drugs, and how he is one of those addicts. He explains by stating, "Say a young cat has someone he respects, looks up to . . . an older man! And say the older man leaves, chases around the country, gets involved with others and ignores his young friend. Then the guy might need a substitute for friendship. He might seek it in junk!"

Rather than have or show any sympathy, Arrow tells Roy that when he hears sob stories like that he wants to lose his lunch, showing just how ignorant he truly is about addiction and its effects.

When Arrow walks Lantern out of the apartment, he returns to see Roy with a syringe full of heroin, shooting up. It's at this point that many of the readers would expect the hero to show compassion for his ward and get him the help he needed to recover from his addiction. Instead, rather than show kindness, sympathy, or compassion, Arrow smacks Roy across the face and tells him that he's no better than the other junkies. Arrow proceeds to kick Roy out of the apartment.

Afterward, Arrow thinks to himself, *Was it me? Did I somehow fail the kid? I haven't paid him much attention lately! But he shouldn't need attention at his age! No, I'm innocent of blame. I've always taught him to be strong, independent, to hang tough!*

Arrow's internal dialogue and his treatment of Roy is evidence of not only how society usually treats addiction, but also how many men view themselves and the problems of their sons. Rather than nurture, care, and understand, many men attempt to work through their emotions. Fathers teach these same strategies to their sons. To help them remain strong and independent, they teach their sons, brothers, and nephews the same lessons of perseverance rather than treatment. When this tactic does not work for these young and adult men, they self-medicate with drugs and alcohol, in the hope that their problems will disappear on their own. Many addicts and men who have been sexually abused are meant to feel shame and guilt for their past or present in the same way as Roy, so they never get the help they deserve. They feel weak, like lesser men, and upset they could not "hang tough."

The story eventually leads to the overdose of one of the kids who mugged Arrow at the beginning of the comic, Arrow and Lantern finding the producers and distributors of the drugs, and Lantern finding Roy going through withdrawal in a back alley. The comic ends with Roy quitting drugs cold turkey and punching Arrow in the face. When asked why he hit him, Roy told Arrow:

Call it sharing! I'm sharing a very small piece of the pain I've just gone through these past few days. The kind of pain thousands of kids are going through every day because an uncaring and unthinking society turns its back on them! Drugs are a symptom and you, like the rest of society, attack the symptom not the disease! But this symptom is worse than most; it maims, it pains, it dims you! It drives you to the edge of sanity and over, with a tag around your toe!

Child sexual abuse is also a disease society has turned its back on, refuses to acknowledge, let alone discuss. It's this disease that leads to drug and alcohol addictions. These comics are not perfect, but they shed light on an issue otherwise ignored in the seventies and even today. Although it made addiction and recovery appear as if it was simply mind over matter, it let other addicts know that addiction can happen to even the best of people, and with the best of intentions, making heroes into villains. However, becoming addicted to drugs and alcohol are temporary fixes that numb the pain you may have, and could lead to a premature death. Any addiction, trauma, or abuse cannot be conquered alone. Find support and lean on those closest until you are able to stand on your own and be the support for someone else. Until then, the cycle will continue. And if you have not become addicted to drugs or alcohol following a traumatic event, consider yourself blessed. Don't judge others and their ability/inability to cope in the same way Arrow judged Roy. This may cause you to become the villain in another person's story. Instead, as Gandhi said, "Be the change you wish to see in the world. It's only then we will all succeed."

Conquering Self-Harm

For some survivors, the pain of their abuse is so great that the only way they believe they can cope with the trauma is through inflicting harm on themselves. Self-mutilation can be done through the cutting of flesh with a knife, scratching scars into the flesh, burning themselves with fire and cigarette butts, or continuously harming themselves in a number of ways. These acts of self-injury create feelings of relief and release from the pain, a sense of control over the abuse, a way to reproduce emotions and feelings that seemed dormant after the abuse, or a way to recreate the abusive situation that was suffered as a child.

It may seem irrational, but in the minds of survivors, the pain caused to the body relieves the pressure of living with the abuse that was suffered sexually, or eliminating the fear of being abused in the future, allowing a few moments of relief in the present. Because of the dark nature of self-inflicting harm, there are not many comic book heroes or villains in the DC universe who inflict harm on themselves instead of others. However, there is one villain in Batman's Rogue Gallery that self-mutilates through the use of slashes into his skin to remember the victims he has killed. His name is Mister Zsasz.

Sometimes the pain of the past can become too much to bear, causing some people to believe the only way to relieve the pain is by hurting themselves with cuts, scratches, self-mutilation, or even suicide. After battling with the depression of losing his parents and the loss of his fortune, Victor Zsasz attempted to commit suicide. However, before succeeding, he realized the pointlessness of life, began killing instead, and with each victim he cut a mark into his skin. Survivors are not killers in the same way as Victor Zsasz, but they yearn for relief of their pain or the opportunity to feel any other emotion rather than fear and depression. Self-harm is a way for them to experience those emotions, no matter how irrational they may appear to others.

Depression, trauma, anxiety, and abuse have different effects on the minds of different people, causing them to react in different ways. For example, when Bruce Wayne's parents were murdered, he responded by fighting a never-ending battle on crime to stop others from experiencing the same loss as he did. Others in the DC universe who suffered the same loss as children or adults did not become as noble. Instead, others such as Victor Zsasz became the villain of their own lives and the lives of others to control the fear and pain of their past.

In *The Batman Chronicles #3*, "The First Cut Is the Deepest," the origins of Victor Zsasz are revealed during a session with his therapist. Here, Zsasz reveals how trauma had a drastic effect on his otherwise normal childhood. He tells his therapist that as a child he had no dysfunctional family background. No trauma. No abuse. He was rich, loved, graduated from college cum laude, but when his parents died in a boating accident, he grew depressed and turned to gambling, eventually losing it all to the Penguin. Broke and depressed, Zsasz, decided there was no longer a reason to live.

He felt nothing and chose to commit suicide by jumping off a bridge. However, before he could succeed he was jumped by a homeless man and threatened with a knife. Rather than give up and succumb to death, both fought for the knife. As they did, Victor came to the realization that all of life was meaningless. After killing the man with the knife, Zsasz thanked him by carving a slash into his skin to feel something and remember that even he was human. From that moment on, Victor Zsasz became Mister Zsasz, the serial killer who often slashed the throats of women, leaving their bodies in lifelike poses, and carving a mark into his skin as a tally to remember the number of his victims.

Self-mutilation allows individuals to feel something, even if it is pain, and remind themselves in the same way as Zsasz, that they are human. Without help and support from those we love, depression can lead to addictions such as gambling and self-harm, in an attempt to forget the past and feel alive.

Although Mister Zsasz is very clearly a psychopathic killer, he reminds Batman of how similar the two are in *Batman #493*, and how easily Batman could have ventured down the same path without support after the death of his parents. Batman responds by nearly beating Mister Zsasz to death, but the villain made an excellent point that Batman refused to accept as truth. After the loss of his parents, Bruce Wayne could have easily become a villain without the help and support of his butler, Alfred, and surrogate mother, Leslie Thompkins. This means that without help, support, and healing after a traumatic event, anyone can begin to venture down the path of self-harm. Survivors of child sexual abuse are no different.

One sexual abuse is not greater or less than another. It only takes one occurrence of sexual abuse to be a survivor, no matter how small it may seem. The primary reason is because, although its effects may not be able to be visible on the surface, like an iceberg most of the pain caused and endured is hidden from view, having lasting negative effects. Just as each sexual abuse is not greater or less severe than another, each lead to different expressions of the same effects of loneliness, isolation, loss of identity, disgrace, pain, fear, and limited emotions. Like all the other coping mechanisms, self-harm is an attempt to relieve those effects and feel normal, loved, wanted, and alive in the same tortured manner as Mister Zsasz.

Although self-harm is severe and can lead to death, like treated wounds you can heal from the sexual abuse of your childhood. As a male survivor of child sexual abuse, no matter what you may have endured or been told, you did not deserve to be abused. You did nothing wrong. You are a good person. You do have self-worth. You make a difference. Fight to remind yourself of this fact every day you open your eyes and breathe another breath. You are not a zombie, but a deserving human being.

Part Three:
Healing

Chapter Thirteen
The Healing Process

The healing process is unique for everyone. This is because no two individuals are the same, and so no two sexual abuses are the same. Throughout the first two parts of this book, there have been attempts to help male survivors of child sexual abuse understand the nature of the trauma they suffered as children and their abilities to cope with it. These two sections were also written to allow male survivors to view themselves in the actions and thoughts of the heroes they honored or villains they despised. However, the primary purpose of this guide has been to help male survivors move toward the path of healing from their sexual abuse, rather than denying it ever took place. The use of superheroes and villains throughout the DC universe was merely used to open the door for discussion of a topic that is viewed by many men and much of society as either taboo or nonexistent. Healing is needed to truly become who you were meant to be.

The healing process is not meant to be a straight line where the survivor moves from start to finish in a set amount of time. When attempting to understand the brain and the effects of trauma, there is no definite beginning, middle, or end. However, there are landmarks. Research has revealed that there are thirteen steps in the healing process of child sexual abuse. The thirteen steps are:

- The decision to heal
- The emergency stage
- Remembering
- Believing it happened
- Breaking silence
- Understanding that it wasn't your fault
- The child within

- Grieving
- Anger
- Disclosures and truth-telling
- Forgiveness
- Spirituality
- Resolution and moving on

Some survivors never go through two of those steps during the healing process: forgiveness and spirituality.

Moving throughout the thirteen steps takes time and requires that each step be continuously revisited at different stages with different insights. Healing cannot take place overnight and cannot be approached as a task in need of being accomplished. The body and mind progress toward healing at their own pace.

Over the course of this journey, life will not come to a stop, because healing does not take place in a vacuum. This means jobs must be worked, children must have parents, and other responsibilities must be met. This creates setbacks, relapses, and a need to revisit stages of the healing process that you may have believed were already met.

Because healing from child sexual abuse is an extremely personal journey, your healing process will be different from any other survivor's. However, as the author of this guide and a male survivor of child sexual abuse, I will attempt to add insight into the healing process through writing exercises that will allow you time to reflect and heal from the effects of your abuse. I will also add support and guidance in completing these exercises by writing and including my own journey through this process, to let you know you are not alone.

As stated previously, there are thirteen steps researchers have found that survivors of child sexual abuse go through in their journey toward healing. However, as a male survivor who has been actively participating in this process with the help of a therapist, psychiatrist, and medication for three years, I discovered that many of the steps I experienced occurred simultaneously rather than separately. The reason for mentioning this is because you may find that your journey is similar.

Many view the healing process as a highway with thirteen separate cities along the way that represent the thirteen steps of healing. In the minds of many, there is a large span of miles between each city where life happens. When a city/step is reached, they believe all that is required is the filling up of gas, getting food, and stopping to see the sights before moving on to the next destination, eventually reaching their new home at the end of a long drive. Rather, the process is more like a river. This river is large and peaceful at times and slim and rough at others. It contains rapids, lulls, and branches into many different smaller streams that flow back into one another. Sometimes these smaller streams can lead out into open ocean, complicating and confusing the journey, causing the voyager to get lost and revisit locations multiple times before getting back on the right path to make their way to their new home.

The parts of this section of the book represent the complicated and confusing nature of the process. However, rather than thirteen separate chapters that represent the thirteen steps of the healing process, I will combine some stages of the healing process, so there are only six, along with writing exercises, to allow exploration of the nature of your abuse with the help of a counselor or therapist. Those six stages are:

- The emergency stage
- The decision to heal
- Breaking silence
- Understanding it wasn't your fault
- Spirituality
- Resolution and moving on

As stated previously, the healing process has no definitive beginning and end. This means that this section of the guide does not have to be read from beginning to end. It should be read and reread slowly, to allow exploration and time for your thoughts to settle on understanding and healing from a specific trauma developed by childhood sexual abuse. Take your time. This is not a race. Start at a section you believe you are ready to handle; put the book down for a while if it has become particularly difficult to read, returning only when you know you are ready. Finally, do not read this section alone. As the author, I have experienced childhood sexual abuse, but I am not a trained therapist, counselor, or psychiatrist trained to address and manage trauma and mental health in the same way they have been trained. Use these pages as a guide to begin the healing process and discussions to overcome the effects of your abuse. You are not alone, so do not attempt this process alone. You are and can be more.

Chapter Fourteen
The Emergency Stage

A hero is an ordinary individual who finds the strength to persevere and endure in spite of overwhelming obstacles.

—Christopher Reeves

The First Step

As a male survivor of child sexual abuse, there may have been, or will be, a time in your life when all you can think of is the sexual abuse you suffered. During this stage, there may be extreme feelings of loneliness, sadness, depression, or anxiety that cannot be controlled or explained. Thoughts of being sexually abused may not be a forethought, because of a denial of the abuse for so many years. There may be moments of crying without warning, shame, and feeling as if everyone knows about the past abuse.

Although this stage of the healing process can best be described as panic, there are also times of remembering and believing that it happened that blend one thought into the other, creating a feeling of insanity, perhaps wanting to commit suicide, do self-harm, or abuse alcohol or drugs. However, during the emergency stage, there is no way to combat the memories of sexual abuse or the feeling of being anxious. Unlike instances that could have been controlled in the past, the emergency stage cannot be pushed away and ignored. The memories and feelings rise to the surface and require attention, no matter what is currently happening in your life or how inconvenient they may be.

There is no way to fully explain the emergency stage or what may be experienced. However, there are strategies to help you get through this stage, no matter how long it takes or how often you return.

Creating a Fortress of Solitude/Batcave

Beneath Wayne Manor and in the depths of the Arctic, both Batman and Superman escaped from the harsh realities of the world they attempted to protect. Batman trained and solved mysteries in the depths of the Batcave, while Superman remained separated from humanity as he explored his Kryptonian heritage in the Fortress of Solitude. While in the emergency stage, and throughout your healing journey, it is important to create a safe place to escape and heal in the same manner as Batman and Superman. This is how I described a safe place as I began my healing journey:

> When we were young, we had our places we went to get away from what was bothering us, somewhere we could sit in peace without siblings or adults having access to us. When we sat down in this safe place we always felt good. It's in this place we were able to play with the objects of childhood. There we could think our thoughts and say our words out loud, without anyone telling us, judging us, or pushing us. That was the wisdom of childhood. Now you can call on that same wisdom. Find or create a safe place for yourself now. A place just for you, not for sharing with anyone else. Your paradise. Spend scheduled time there at first. In the future, you will be drawn to your safe space naturally. There you can rest, heal, hide, think, play, and get yourself ready to go back out and be your best.

Creating a safe place is vital to your recovery. It is in this place that you will meditate, reflect, and center yourself. Without this safe place, there can be no true growth and inner peaPreviously, in the section on heroes, Willie Fawcett explained in *Superman #276* how he had no memory of how he got to Metropolis or what happened when he became Captain Thunder. Joseph Kerr and Harvey Dent suffered the same lapses of memory in the villains portion of this guide in *Batman: Legends of the Dark Knight #66* and "The Eye of the Beholder." Gradually, over time, all three individuals began to regain the pieces of their memory they believed had been lost due to traumatic events. Some memories were good, others were bad, but all were vital to proper healing. These memories began to return due to events they saw and heard, through objects that where given to them, or simply due to the passage of time.

During and after the emergency stage, memories of childhood sexual abuse may fade and return in the same way as the previously mentioned characters. These memories are different from others acquired from day to day. Nonthreatening memories have no problem being recollected with no serious strain. However, the memories of sexual abuse have the same effects on the mind and body as other traumatic events, such as mass shootings, bombings, natural disasters, and hostage situations. The only major and devastating difference is that survivors of child sexual abuse cannot share the memories of their experience with fellow survivors of the same traumatic event to verify the memory's accuracy. The reason for this is because child sexual abuse happens in secret, behind closed doors, while being told to never tell. The secrets of sexual abuse create soldiers of a war only sexual abuse survivors are allowed to discuss. In many circumstances, the only other person knowledgeable of the abuse to discuss the accuracy of these memories with is the perpetrator. The inability to verify these traumatic memories is why many male survivors doubt they were ever truly sexual abused to begin with.

Remembering the abuse varies for each survivor. Some individuals can remember details of their abuse with little problem, while remaining distant and numb to feelings. Others may remember fragments of pieces or nothing at all. This is normal, mostly because children dissociate from their bodies during sexual abuse, in the same way Willie Fawcett and Harvey Dent dissociated from their bodies to manage their pain, creating instances of traumatic amnesia.

The surfacing of these memories cannot be controlled during the emergency stage. For many survivors, memories of their sexual abuse may seem to happen without explanation, appearing in vivid dreams and nightmares in the same way horrific terrors of a bat and killer clown haunted Joseph Kerr. However, the flashback of memories can occur for a number of reasons. Some of these reasons may be:

- **Triggers**: Certain smells, touches, a familiar sound from the past, internal sensations, or visual images may trigger a flashback of a sexual abuse. These are recalled through sense memories the body has held on to even if the mind has tried to push them away.

- **Quitting Addictions**: As discussed in "Villains," through the addiction of heroin by Green Lantern's sidekick, Speedy, addictions to drugs and alcohol are coping mechanisms to sometimes deal with the trauma of childhood sexual abuse. After quitting an addiction, memories that were once repressed are now allowed to be remembered.

- **Life-Changing Events**: As discussed in "Heroes," when Barry Allen was resurrected after his death, the thought of his mother's death was all he could think of. The life changing event of cheating death brought dormant memories to the surface. Other life-changing events have the same effect on survivors as resurrection from the Speed Force had on Barry. Some common life-changing events include becoming a parent, the death of a family member, being robbed or vandalized, getting married, or experiencing a natural disaster such as a fire or earthquake. All of these can cause memories of child sexual abuse to surface.

- **Becoming Safe:** Being sexually abused as a child meant never truly feeling safe. Often, adults may have been viewed as individuals who could not be trusted. This meant protecting emotions and limiting access to feelings, in the same manner Bruce Wayne suppressed his emotions after the murder of his parents. However, as an adult, if a safe environment is created, over time the mind and body will allow emotions to become unhindered and memories to surface.

- **Visuals**: Watching news coverage, movies, or videos may trigger memories of your own sexual abuse.

In *Detective Comics #633*, "Identity Crisis," discussed in the hypervigilance portion of the section in villains, Bruce Wayne/The Synaptic Kid felt as though he was losing control of his life with each revelation that he was no longer Batman. He felt as though someone or something else limited his actions and identity like a puppet on marionette strings. Throughout the emergency stage, you may have a similar experience. It may feel as though the memories have control over your life and who you are, rather than the other way around. However, over time the memories will no longer be viewed as a curse, causing unexplainable bouts of misery and sadness. Given enough time, patience, and support from a trained counselor or therapist, the pieces of your past abuse will begin to fit together to provide understanding and healing.

If you push the memories away, as may have been the practice in the past, during the emergency stage the memories will surface in the form of exhaustion, nightmares, and depression, the same as Joseph Kerr as he pushed away the memories of the Joker, or it could cause migraines, anxiety, and uncontrollable dissociative episodes that may take the form of vivid daydreams in the same manner as Harvey Dent in the courtroom. Denying your mind and body access to these memories will take their toll if not dealt with properly.

What must be remembered with each flashback and trigger is that it will not last forever. Over time, as progress is made throughout this stage of the healing process, you will notice the days and seasons change just as before.

Believing It Happened

As discussed in "Villains," Lex Luthor denies his role as a villain. Through his eyes, he is a savior—and for a while he was. The people of Lexor worshipped him as the savior of their planet. However, continued denial of his role in hurting others, and a refusal to properly heal from his past, made Lex run away and attempt to forget the actions of his past. In doing so, he reverted to his previous ways, destroying his entire world and leaving him with nothing but an unquenchable desire for revenge and continued denial of his role as a villain.

In the same way denial had a devastating impact on Lex Luthor, denial can have an impact on a survivor's understanding of themselves and their abuse. It may not cause an entire planet to explode, but the effects may feel that way if not treated.

Denial may have been, or still is, a large part of the way in which you cope as a male survivor of child sexual abuse. One primary reason for the denial that any sexual abuse ever took place is because of the views of sexual abuse held by society. Most individuals believe, whether they are male or female, that men and boys cannot be raped. This is especially true if the perpetrator is an older, attractive female. It is believed that if sexual abuse does occur to a male it only happens to homosexuals. Very rarely, if ever, does it occur to heterosexual men. However, the truth is much more startling. One in every six men are sexually abused in their lifetime. This sexual abuse occurs to all men and boys, regardless of sexual preferences, by other men, boys, girls, and women.

Second, denial of sexual abuse for many male survivors is the only way they believe their manhood can be retained. Acknowledgement of rape, incest, or other sexual abuse by a male often makes them believe they can no longer call themselves men without causing questions and conflicting thoughts about what it means to be a man. Men who have been sexually abused as boys must also acknowledge their weakness as children to protect themselves, and this may cause conflicting thoughts that because they were weak in the past they are weak now.

There are many reasons males deny their sexual abuse as children. Unfortunately, knowing and accepting childhood sexual abuse is the only way to progress through the stages of healing and exit the emergency stage.

For many males, remembering, acknowledging, and trusting the memories of their childhood sexual abuse is almost an impossibility, not only because of their own thoughts, but also because of the beliefs of male role models. The consistent rhetoric from older males to sons, siblings, nephews, cousins, and grandchildren when a boy states their abuse is that "nothing happened," "put it in the past," "move on," and "that could never happen." This is especially true if the abuse occurred by another male or family member.

However, the rhetoric changes entirely if the sexual abuse of a male occurs at the hands of a female. Rather than negative, this form of sexual abuse may be viewed as positive by other males and praised. This is because sex is viewed as the highest priority for "real men," along with being a sign of fertility and manhood, while creating the illusion that any sexual encounter with an attractive or older female should be wanted. When these thoughts and beliefs are perpetuated by male role models and others throughout communities and society, male survivors feel as though their memory cannot be trusted. This creates a need to deny they were ever sexually abused or that they did not initiate it. Believing it happened may be especially difficult for male survivors, because they may continuously believe they do not exist and that men cannot be raped. Although this belief may appear to be the truth among other men and society, as a male survivor you must know and believe that if a sexual encounter was not wanted it was sexual abuse.

Others may doubt the nature of male sexual abuse because of beliefs and stereotypes they hold, but the denial of your memories will only lead to more confusion and a refusal to heal from the trauma. Believe and accept the memories and emotions as they return through triggers and flashbacks. Eventually, you will begin to trust the nature of your memories as they continue to weave together and create a full view of the abuse you suffered, helping you heal from the trauma and become a complete person.

Strategies to Remember and Believe You Were Abused

Memories of your sexual abuse and the trauma you survived cannot be controlled during the emergency stage. Triggers occur throughout the day without warning or explanation, causing flashbacks. Although memories of the abuse may not be able to be controlled, sometimes they can be sensed as they begin to rise and take shape. When this occurs, there are measures that you can take to reduce their impact on your daily routine:

- **Get Safe**: If you are home, go to your safe place. If you are at work, find a place where you can be alone and feel safe, like a portable Batcave that can be used as a safe house. If you are in public, find a place where you can ride out the memory until it passes. If possible, do not drive.

- **Embrace the Memory:** Relax and let the memory come. Do not try and fight it. Refusing to accept the memory will only lead to dissociative episodes like those experienced and discussed through the fictional characters Joseph Kerr and Harvey Dent in the villains portion of the book. This means do not stifle the memory through alcohol, drugs, or food. If possible, take notes during or after the memory in your journal to help you understand how it fits into the understanding of the sexual abuse.

- **It's A Memory, Not A Recurrence**: Know that the memory you are having is not the actual abuse that occurred in the past. Unlike the original trauma, this memory cannot hurt you. Know that you are safe.

- **Know You Are Strong**: Experiencing memories of past abuse often brings a cascade of emotions and anxiety that may cause feelings of being weak and less of a man. Know that having emotions such as anxiety, sadness, fear, and depression do not make you a lesser human being. You are not a superhero or an evil villain. Use their stories and archetypes for guidance, but do not strive to emulate their behavior. The characters used throughout this book are fictional, but you are an individual with needs, wants, and emotions the same as anyone else. Do not have shame in feeling weak and vulnerable. Instead, take this time to provide yourself with needed self-care, and take pride in knowing you are healing from past wounds to become stronger.

- **Take Time**: Do not rush the memory or the emotions that come rushing afterward. If the memory has drained needed energy, take the needed time to heal before moving forward and continuing with the day.

- **Talk**: The memory may bring shame, but it is important to no longer need to hide the abuse you suffered as a child. Share your emotions, thoughts, and fears with a loved one, therapist, counselor, or yourself by writing the memory in your journal.

These memories may raise questions about whether you were truly sexually abused, and whether you could have been sexually abused because you were a boy at the time. This doubt is normal, and the questions it raises are similar for male and female survivors. It is important to not deny these questions or your sexual abuse. Acknowledge these questions, but do not rush to get answers. Explore and discuss them with the people supporting you throughout this journey. The abuse from childhood can create holes in your memory that need more time to patch the memories of the abuse together.

Throughout this process, it is important to know and accept that you are not crazy. Trust yourself, your thoughts, and your emotions. You know yourself best, no matter what others may say or the doubts they may have. You are strong. You are a survivor.

Strategies for Surviving the Emergency Stage

Although there is no way to prevent living through the emergency stage if you are a survivor of child sexual abuse, to keep the memories of your abuse from occurring through flashback, or minimize the effects of no longer denying the sexual abuse, there are techniques that can help relieve the anxiety and stress of progressing through this stage of the healing process.

- **Find people you can talk to.** Create a support staff you can trust that will not judge your past or minimize your feelings. While it is important to create a safe place, you cannot spend all your time in your Fortress of Solitude during the emergency stage. Instead, you must venture out and live your life through this trying time.

- **Seek a counselor/therapist.** You are not alone, so do not take on the task of attempting to heal without help. Finding a trained professional who specializes in sexual abuse trauma will help reassure you that the emotions and thoughts you are having are real and justified. This will provide hope and reassurance that you are not going crazy. Receiving help does not make you weak. Even superheroes have sidekicks.

- **Seek medication.** Batman is purely an idea. While Bruce Wayne may have learned to cope with the passing of his parents by traveling the globe and learning to battle crime, you live in the real world. Do not believe suffering the traumatic event of childhood sexual abuse does not include the possibility of getting help to handle overwhelming emotions and thoughts. Medication is not right for everyone, but it may help relieve symptoms of anxiety and depression, not dull them away. Consult a doctor to find out if this is a good fit.

- **Do something spiritual.** Prayer and connecting to your religion can provide strength and support when it is needed.

- **Create a list of activities that calm you down.** Some activities you may include are working out, listening to music you have placed on a playlist designed specifically for moments of anxiety, watching your favorite movie, going for a walk or run, or writing in your journal. When overwhelmed, take some time to visit your list and do something for yourself.

Healing Exercise: Meditation

A strategy that is helpful throughout all stages of the healing process is learning to meditate. Meditation allows time for thoughts to mature, the mind to rest, and the body to relax. To many, beginning it seems impossible, but like all other activities it takes practice to master. To understand different meditation techniques, you may want to seek out classes, research, and watch videos on the Internet to master this developing skill. As you begin this process, it is important to know that there is no goal to be reached. Instead, meditation requires a calm mind. Below are three different meditation strategies you can use:

- **Stairs:**

  Create a safe place.

  While in your safe place, sit comfortably for fifteen minutes. If you feel comfortable doing so, play relaxing sounds for meditation. For example, nature sounds of crashing waves or falling rain.

  Close your eyes and breathe slowly. Take deep breaths in through your nose and out through your mouth.

  Picture ten steps in your mind. These steps can be of any style you feel comfortable imagining.

  Imagine numbers on each step descending from ten at the top to one at the bottom. The color of the paint and steps is your choice.

  See yourself carefully walking backward down each step one at a time.

  As you descend, continue to breathe deeply in through your nose and out through your mouth. With each step, you should feel yourself becoming more at rest and your mind at ease.

When you reach the bottom of the steps, continue to breathe while allowing your mind to wander and unwind on its own for the remainder of the fifteen minutes.

At the end of the fifteen minutes, slowly ascend the steps until you return to your body.

- **Progressive Relaxation:**

  Create a safe place.

  While in your safe place, sit comfortably for fifteen minutes. If you feel comfortable doing so, play relaxing sounds for meditation. For example, nature sounds of crashing waves or falling rain.

  Close your eyes and breathe slowly. Take deep breaths in through your nose and out through your mouth.

  Very slowly, beginning at your toes, tense your muscles. Do this very slowly, all the way to the top of your head.

  Slowly relax your muscles, starting at your head all the way down to your toes.

  Repeat tensing and relaxing your muscles for the remainder of the fifteen minutes (at least three to five times.)

- **Neon Light:**

  Create a safe place.

  While in your safe place, sit comfortably for fifteen minutes. If you feel comfortable doing so, play relaxing sounds for meditation. For example, nature sounds of crashing waves or falling rain.

  Close your eyes and breathe slowly. Take deep breaths in through your nose and out through your mouth.

  Imagine a neon ring. The color of the ring is your choice.

  Imagine the neon ring loosely encircling your ankles. The ring does not hurt but has a sense of healing radiating outward and into your skin.

Slowly imagine the neon ring extending up your body, expanding and retracting to match the shape and form of your body as it moves all the way to your head. As it moves, imagine the warmth radiating from the glow of the ring and into your body.

Once the ring reaches your head, imagine it slowly moving down your body, healing as it moves.

Continue to imagine the neon ring slowly moving up and down your body, healing as it does for the remainder of the fifteen minutes.

At the end of the fifteen minutes, do an activity you enjoy or that soothes you. Some activities may be:

- Sleep
- Exercise
- Read
- Take a shower
- Talk to someone for support
- Pray
- Cry

Writing Exercise #1: Remembering

Remembering the nature of your sexual abuse is difficult, no matter who the survivor may be. However, knowing you were sexually abused and remembering you were sexually abused is difficult. Pieces of the abuse may come out at separate times, and rather than memories, you may experience physical sensations. Piecing these memories together will help you understand and accept that men and boys can be the victim of childhood sexual abuse. Writing the memories in a journal throughout the emergency stage will help in your healing to verify your emotions and that this did happen to you.

Below is the story of my sexual abuse as a male survivor. It is included to help you as a male survivor know you are not alone. This story was originally published in *Raped Black Male: A Memoir*.

Men Can't Be Raped

I wish I had a better memory of what occurred the first time I was raped, but it's been over twenty years and some of the memories have become hazy. I do know the house was empty of my parents and brother. What's interesting is that the first time wasn't the first time. It began with my abuser and a pornographic tape. My abuser was my sister and, at the time, babysitter. I would often have a babysitter when Mom had to work late at K-Mart, or Dad went out and had to DJ at The American Legion. My parents also simply went out sometimes (as parents should), or they didn't get home from work until after 5 p.m. when I got out of school and home about 3:15/3:30. So, during that time, when we were alone, is when the grooming began.

Knowing and understand grooming is not what you may think. It's not when two individuals sit down and brush and comb the other's hair like chimps in a zoo. Grooming is a term used to explain how abusers prepare their victim for molestation. For some abusers, it occurs when their victim runs around, becoming excited while playing tag, for example. Then, instead of the abuser tagging their victim, the abuser grabs the genitals, breasts, or puts their hands down the victim's pants. Anything to get the child sexual aroused and excited while making their victim believe they are safe and participating in fun game. Afterward, the roles are reversed. The abuser has the victim run, tag, and touch them in the same way. This makes the victim believe this is how the game is played, and allows the abuser to open the door to more egregious acts and games where the abuser can easily sexually assault with less resistance and more severity.

My grooming occurred in the form of pornographic movies.

My dad had a collection of pornographic videocassettes under the mattress of the bed in the basement of our home that were easily accessible and could easily be replaced after they were used as if they were never touched. Eventually, after the basement had been remodeled and the bed and mattress were thrown in the trash, the cassettes were moved to the bottom drawer of the desk in the basement.

The reason I remember this bed so vividly is because me, my sister, and Daniel would often play on the mattress when my parents were gone. Both would have me lay on the mattress while they would run and jump on the bed to try and fling me into the air and against the wall. I loved it. Just crazy, stupid, innocent stuff kids do when their parents are gone—unlike what eventually happened when Daniel moved away after physical fighting with my father.

The grooming began one afternoon when my parents were gone. I was being babysat, and she asked with a calm, happy smile after entering my room, "Hey Kenny, wanna see something cool?" Of course, I agreed. I was eight years old. I lived for cool. Cool was my life, and she knew it.

From my room, she led me down to the basement, lifted the mattress, removed the black cassette tape, and placed it in the VCR. I remember that the cassette wasn't labeled as pornography, instead it had a normal white label on the spine of the cassette, as if it had once been a different movie that had been taped over. Because it looked like so many other movies in our library, I never suspected the contents the movie actually contained.

Like most movies in the 80s and 90s paused in the middle of the cassette, it didn't start at the beginning. Instead, it continued from the last moment my father hit stop, which was in the middle of two people moving, groaning, humping, and fitting pieces of their body into places I had no idea was possible at such an age. Immediately, I was disgusted. At the time, I didn't know what it was, but I knew it was a movie I was not supposed to watch.

My eight-year-old brain flashed back to scenes of Spike Lee's *School Daze* and how my parents told me to cover my eyes during the "dirty parts." Seeing what was happening on the screen, I figured this was most definitely a dirty part I wasn't allowed to watch, so I covered my eyes and waited for the okay that the scene had ended and I could open my eyes to something safe. Instead, she took my hands from my eyes and said, "Watch. It's funny." I tried to cover my eyes during a few scenes that followed that were especially embarrassing, but I was coaxed into watching.

Soon it was over. When it came to an end, she rewound the tape to where it began, put the cassette under the mattress, and went back upstairs to continue the day. Nothing happened. She did not try and touch me, or me to touch her. Rather than grooming me to become sexually aroused through a game that allowed us to explore the other's body, she groomed me to like the idea of sex through the use of movies, which were a primary source of entertainment in our house. Any free moment the family had was spent watching a movie. We all had our classic repeats we could (and did) watch over and over again. My mother loved *Toy Soldiers*, *The Five Heartbeats*, and *The Temptations*. Daniel loved *The Last Dragon*. I loved *The Rocketeer* and *Hook*, and my dad simply loved movies in general. Going to Blockbuster on Friday evenings to search the shelves for a new release or an unwatched classic was always on the agenda. Because movies were such a large part of the lives in my family, my abuser had found an in that made grooming through pornographic movies safe, fun, and a common form of entertainment that my eight-year-old self would never question as not being valid and acceptable.

Of course, I knew not to tell about watching the videos. I was never told not to tell, but I just knew. Technically, nothing had happened, and I had been groomed after years of breaking figurines, rules, and going places when my parents left, that what happened when they were gone was not allowed to be discussed unless we were caught. Then, and only then, was I allowed to sing like a bird. It ensured no one got in trouble. Unfortunately, my abuser never got caught.

For months, this is how it went. My parents would leave, she'd get the tape from under the mattress, we'd watch, put it back, and continued with our day, never saying a word to our parents. The only other person to tell that could have stopped the abuse from happening was Daniel, who was eighteen years old at the time, out of high school and attending Alabama A&M in Huntsville, Alabama. Eventually, Daniel dropped out of college after the first year, joined the military, and moved to Germany to raise a family of his own, making him completely unavailable until my early teens. Although the grooming lasted for many months, it eventually turned to something much more sinister.

As time progressed and the grooming continued, my abuser and I no longer sat on the floor together watching the video in silence, disgust, or mock laughter. Instead, each of us had our own positions in the room, separate from the other. She lay on the bed with a comforter over her body, while I sat on the couch and watched the scenes play out on the screen. After months of watching the cassette in secret on weekends, or late nights when our parents were gone, I no longer covered my eyes and looked away in embarrassment. In fact, most times I had become sexually aroused. My therapist tells me it's normal because it's a natural reaction of the body after being stimulated by the brain, but I find it hard to not view myself as a protagonist of the sex and abuse, no matter what she tells me. However, I did not masturbate. Mostly because I had no idea what masturbation was or that it was even possible. I was too young to know. My abuser, on the other hand, being five years my senior, was discovering masturbation beneath the comforter on the mattress ten feet away from where I sat while watching a woman receive pleasure from a man in the same way she sexually stimulated herself.

After being groomed to willingly watch pornography while remaining silent of the molestation, becoming sexual aroused, and her being sexually stimulated through masturbation, all the pieces had fallen into place for me to be raped with little resistance—and that's precisely what occurred.

The first time grooming transgressed to rape, my abuser called me to the bed where she lay with the blanket pulled over her body from where I sat on the couch. I looked at the bed and walked over. She said calmly but with a little hesitation, "Let's try something different. Get on top of me." This is when she pulled back the blanket to reveal she had on no pants or panties.

Immediately, I froze. I had no idea what to say or do. I thought to myself, *Is this okay? Can I say no?* I wanted to say no, but I didn't know how. How could I? She was someone I trusted. I thought I had to do what she said. She was my sister. I believed with all my heart, beyond a shadow of a doubt, she wouldn't do anything to hurt me. It's taken nearly thirty years, therapy, and meditation for this belief to finally change.

In the moment, she noticed my hesitation. Seeing all those thoughts run through my head at once, she knew she couldn't give me an option. With more confidence, invitingly but with more force, she said, "Let's do what they do. Come on," as she worked off my pants.

When the rape happened and she placed me on top of her, I didn't move. I lay there, lifeless, uncomfortable, and cold. She was larger, and there was no way for me to touch the mattress, so I lay hovering in the air on top and inside her body as the pornographic movie continued to play in the background. When I didn't move, she became frustrated and annoyed that I wasn't doing it right. Again, she took control over the situation, grabbed me by the waist and made me move up and down, in and out, as she watched the scenes play out on the screen on the other side of the room. It lasted only a few minutes, but the impact has yet to vanish. She finished and I stopped moving. We both got dressed, she rewound the tape, put it back under the mattress as always, but this time was different. Rather than go upstairs to continue our day, she said what she had never said before: don't tell.

"It's bad," she said, "and we'll get in trouble."

I was too young to argue or know what it meant, so I didn't tell. I remained silent, just as she wanted. For over twenty years I remained quiet, because I didn't want to get in trouble. I thought, it was my fault and I'd be punished. There was nothing I could do if I didn't want Mom, Dad, and Daniel to look at me with the shame and regret I felt. I had done something wrong that no one knew had occurred except her, so the best and only option was to keep quiet, never tell, and keep her secret.

How did this make me feel? In the moment, I felt dirty. I curled up inside myself, waiting for it to stop, and I haven't stopped waiting. I didn't say much. There was no kissing or fondling, just sex. And that's how it went for almost two years. Our parents would leave, pornography would play, I would be raped, and I wouldn't tell. Over time, I began to anticipate when it was going to happen, even look forward to it. My therapist says this is natural. She says it's normal to have been aroused and sexually stimulated. It's something the body does and something I couldn't control, but it still doesn't change what I feel, and that is that it was my fault. That I could have stopped it. That I enjoyed it. That I'm to blame, and that no matter what I do I'm damned, with no amount of forgiveness that can bring me back.

Then, without warning, one day, abruptly, the rapes stopped. After church she told me, almost out of the blue, we couldn't do it anymore because it was wrong and that it never happened. I said okay, but my mind was racing. One thought after the other came without stop. "You did this to me and now you're saying we can't do it anymore? *And* you're telling me it never happened? You're telling me it was wrong? How wrong was it? Why was it wrong? What's going to happen to me if someone finds out?" It wasn't until much later that I would find answers to any of these questions.

You may be wondering why the rapes abruptly came to an end. I have wondered the same question. I believed for years that she came to an epiphany that what she was doing psychologically, physically, and morally damaging to someone she was supposed to love and protect, when the truth is much more logical and hurtful. I had become too old and was no longer useful. In two years, when this all began, I had gone from an eight-year-old child to a ten-year-old prepubescent boy with the possibility of getting my fifteen-year-old sister pregnant. Pregnancy meant being discovered, and this was something she could not allow to happen, so she told me it was wrong and brought it to an end, leaving me broken and confused with no understanding that incest had occurred, while allowing the thought that would mature into a belief that would eventually become a cold, hard fact: men can't be raped.

Writing Exercise #2: Knowing You're Not Superman

As mentioned in the previous section on heroes, as a male survivor, you may have felt the need to hold the world on your shoulders and be Superman. However, throughout the emergency stage you may come to realize just how vulnerable you are. This may mean overextending yourself and falling short of reaching your goal when you take on too many responsibilities. In the same way Superman was discussed as having low self-esteem when he is unable to accomplish everything, your self-esteem may be affected as you journey through the healing process, requiring needed self-care rather than prolonged mental abuse by viewing yourself as inadequate and incapable of accomplishing everything.

To complete this writing exercise, think about your past and remember a time you attempted to do more than you were capable of accomplishing. Write about how it made you feel, your thoughts at the time, and what happened afterward. This event can be during the emergency stage of your healing process or at an earlier time.

The event described below is from my own journal. When my brother-in-law TJ passed away in 2016, I attempted to be Superman, and the effects devastated my self-esteem, leading to depression, anxiety, and thoughts of suicide.

TJ

In the fall of 2016, my brother-in-law TJ fell sick, was remitted into hospice, and passed away two weeks afterward at the age of twenty-eight. TJ was born with the degenerative brain disease known as MPS, or Sanfillipo syndrome. It is rare, but detrimental in its effects.

As a boy, TJ was fully functional as a toddler. He could run, talk, eat, and play in most ways as any other toddler. However, as he grew older, his motor functions, speech, and mobility became limited, until he was implanted with a feeding tube and limited in movement to either his wheelchair or bed. Unfortunately, MPS strikes quickly in most children who are diagnosed with the disease. Most never live to see their teens, and almost certainly never reach the age of twenty. So, for TJ to live almost to his thirties is testament to his drive to live, the people around him who loved him, and the lives he touched.

When TJ fell sick and it was evident he was not going to get better, Sarah, my wife, and my two children, Mirus and Amare, made our way to Wooster, Ohio, to be with him in his final days. Sarah spent her time in the hospice with her younger brother and parents. For over a week, TJ fought, refusing to let go within an inch of his life and struggling to breathe. As he rallied day after day, my mother and father-in-law made the decision to take TJ home where he and the rest of the family would be more comfortable.

During the week TJ was in hospice, I was taking care of Mirus and Amare, leaving and returning to hospice when it seemed TJ was able to handle visitors, to ensure everyone was allowed to take care of themselves and mourn the losing of TJ. However, as the days of isolation spent in the home of my in-laws slowly crept forward, dealing with two toddler girls out of the element of our own home, while remaining supportive to Sarah as she watched her brother wither away, began to take its toll.

When TJ left hospice and returned home, I believed the entire family would make our way back to Baltimore, Maryland, then return at a moment's notice to be with TJ in his last hours. However, Sarah made the decision to stay, and I agreed that it was the best decision. To ensure she did not have to worry about the girls, I decided to take them back to Baltimore with me.

At the time, I believed I could drive through the night on Sunday as Mirus and Amare slept, sleep a few hours at home, get the girls dressed and to daycare before getting to work to teach a full day with a class of seventh graders. I believed I was Superman. I could do it all. However, driving through the night and waking up the next morning to a house absent of Sarah as my brother-in-law passed away in Ohio was too much. I was able to get the girls dressed and to daycare, but I could not get to work. I spent the day sleeping, cleaning, and beating myself up for not being with my wife and not making it to work.

I was able to attend work the next day, but cried the entire drive after taking Mirus and Amare to daycare. I spoke to my mother on the phone for support, but when I arrived I broke down. The thought of preparing to teach seventh graders, all the work that needed to be accomplished at school and at home, on top of feeling like a shitty husband and son-in-law, was too much. Tears came uncontrollably as I began to have returning thoughts of suicide. I asked my principal for a long-term substitute for my class, but was told my absences were a burden to my other seventh-grade team members, so I stayed. I also was not sure if I would have tried to act out my thoughts of suicide if I went home.

The next morning, TJ passed. I took my daughters to daycare, taught throughout the day, raced home to pack our bags, picked up Mirus and Amare, and drove the six hours through the night back to Wooster, Ohio.

Like Superman, I refused to admit my own weaknesses and shortcomings. Instead, I tried to do it all, failed, and hated myself for it, because as a survivor I believed I needed to be perfect and accomplish everything I planned. This is because of a penetrating fear of losing the world I had built for myself and my family. I must have a sense of control and safety that was stripped away from me when I was raped. I had no way of accomplishing it all; my self-esteem suffered. As a survivor of child sexual abuse, I must know and accept what I can and cannot do if I want to continue to heal and stay mentally healthy. Sometimes, pushing myself beyond my comfort zone helps me to succeed and become a better man. However, other times it holds me back, damaging me through negative thoughts. The key is to know when to push and when to rest.

Chapter Fifteen
The Decision to Heal

A hero is someone who has given his or her life to something bigger than oneself.

—Joseph Campbell

Making the Choice

In Joseph Campbell's 1949 book, *The Hero With A Thousand Faces*, the author explores the similarities of hero myths across the world and throughout the ages. Through his exploration in the book, he makes the argument that all heroes have the same defining characteristics that mark the progression of their voyage called the "hero's journey." This progression voyage of the hero can be mapped step-by-step in the stories of Jesus all the way to *Harry Potter* and *Star Wars*. It can even by seen in the journey toward healing documented by researchers of child sexual abuse and in this book.

The first step in the hero's journey is the departure from their home and familiar territory to places unknown to begin their adventure. It is here the hero receives the "call to adventure." This is the occurrence of an incident that requires the formation of a hero to rise and meet a challenge. This could be the kidnapping of a princess, the rise of an ancient evil from the past, or a disaster that puts innocent lives in danger. Next, the hero recognizes their need, but instead decides to do nothing. The hero believes the problem does not concern them or is too difficult to be accomplished. This is called the "refusal to the call." Although the hero refuses the task placed before them, fate interjects to ensure the hero fulfills their destiny. When fate interjects, it provides supernatural aid or the destruction of the heroes known world to cause them to cross the first threshold and begin their adventure.

Although Joseph Campbell was referring to the journey of heroes in literature, the same steps can be applied to the journey of healing. The emergency stage is the survivor's call to adventure.

Next is the decision to heal. This is the same as the hero's choice to either continue along the journey or not. This means that you, as a survivor, have the choice of continuing along the journey to heal, or not. Choosing to not continue your journey may appear to be an easier option, but it can lead to your own destruction and sadness.

Researchers have found that, for many survivors, the decision to heal comes before the emergency stage. However, as a male survivor of child sexual abuse, I can understand how the emergency stage is what may have led you to acknowledge your own sexual abuse. The emergency stage may have occurred during a time when it felt that the sexual abuse as a child had been pushed away and dealt with, only to arise and attack without reason. For some male survivors, this may have occurred after a major life-changing event, discussed in the chapter on the emergency stage. Unfortunately, it may also have been after quitting an alcohol or drug addiction, or from the fear of the man you were becoming as others closest to you warned of your thoughts and actions transforming into those of a villain. No matter the reason, because of the impact of societal expectations and views of male sexuality, the emergency stage may have been the cause for beginning this journey of healing.

Although this may be true, the decision still has to be made to continue to heal from the trauma of childhood sexual abuse or to continue to deny any abuse, suppress the memories, and self-medicate with the use of drugs and alcohol. Making this decision is not easy. It requires questioning many beliefs about the classic definition of what it means to be a man, allowing vulnerability to be explored, expressing dormant emotions, revealing secrets that may be difficult for others to hear, and coming to the realization that you are only human.

This decision to heal requires strength and understanding that it will not be easy; it requires hard work. Although making the decision to heal may be difficult, that journey is deserving of every survivor. It is life-changing, spiritual, and deeply moving, but a decision no one else but you can make. It means taking back control of a life that was taken as a child, allowing you to become a complete person.

Writing Exercise #3: Your Hero Code

Everyone has a code that they live by, even if it is never stated or written. This code guides the actions and beliefs of individuals. For some it may change slightly over time, but without understanding the code and how to change it, at its core it will remain the same.

In the section on heroes and the hero code, this was discussed in reference to the Flash. As a male survivor of child sexual abuse, your code may be similar to Barry's and consist of absolute thoughts and black-and-white thinking. Although this view of the world may have allowed you to survive the trauma of your sexual abuse as a child, as an adult it can lead to the transformation from becoming the hero of your own story to becoming the villain of others. As a child, it may have provided a source of strength, but over time the coping strategies may lose their needed effects.

Take the opportunity in your journal to explore your own hero code as you make the decision to heal. Explore the views of yourself, the world, and others with your therapist or counselor. It will allow both of you to see evidence of some form of the absolute thinking you have developed.

Over time, as you move through the healing process, your code will change and the absolute thoughts you held at the beginning of the process should change, as your brain begins to heal from the trauma of being sexually abused. When you feel you have made strides in your journey toward healing, rewrite your code. Take notice of the differences, discuss them with your therapist or counselor, and praise your achievements. No matter what, every survivor deserves to heal—even you.

Below is my hero code at the beginning of my journey and how it has changed over the last three years.

My Hero Code Then

- I don't need anyone's help. I can do any and everything on my own if I really try.

- People can't be trusted to be there when you need them. Eventually, given enough time, everyone lets you down. It's best to learn not to depend on anyone in the first place.

- I don't need to rest. If I push myself, I can keep going.

- I have to be happy. If I'm not happy then I'm sad or angry. There is no middle ground.

- I have a plan and I'm sticking to it.

- If I don't keep working and moving I am going to lose everything.

- I'm not strong enough.

- I have to be strong enough.

- Everyone is depending on me.

- It's all my fault.

- I have to be perfect.

My Hero Code Now

Everyone is responsible for his or her own actions. It is my job to be the best version of myself I can be. This means doing what I *want* to do, not what I *have* to do. This does not mean being perfect or shirking my responsibilities, but it does mean knowing I have limits and self-worth. Realizing I have limitations does not make me weak. In fact, it makes me better, because it reminds me that I was unable to stop my abuse as a child and that I am strong now. Knowing, acknowledging, and accepting that I was sexually abused as a child does not mean blaming others for my abuse, but holding people accountable for their actions. I am a good person. And no matter what others may say (including my own inner voice), it was not my fault. Men can be raped.

My Hero Code Differences: Then and Now

I have learned throughout this process (sometimes kicking and screaming as my therapist drags me along) to not be so hard on myself, that having emotions and leaning on others for support is not a sign of weakness, that loving someone does not mean to not hold him or her accountable for their actions. What I continue to struggle in understanding and knowing is that the abuse was not my fault because I was the boy and she was the girl. I will learn to believe the statement that it wasn't my fault as it weaves its way through my code, binding it together.

Chapter Sixteen
Breaking the Silence

Show me a hero and I'll write you a tragedy.

—F. Scott Fitzgerald

Why Speak?

Revealing the nature of childhood sexual abuse is difficult for any survivor. However, talking about your own sexual abuse may be especially difficult because of societal stigmas of males as perpetuators of rape and women as victims. Although the idea of revealing the nature of your sexual abuse to those closest to you may seem to be an impossibility, deciding to tell someone is crucial to the healing process. The primary reason that telling is so pivotal is because when survivors make the decision to no longer be silent, a portion of the control and power that was taken when they were victimized is returned. Although you may have wanted to break the silence about your abuse many times in the past, there may have been reasons you never spoke or were never believed.

Why You May Have Remained Silent

As a child, you may have wanted to tell about your sexual abuse. You may have even told others but were not believed. You may have been told, "that's impossible" or "that can't happen to boys; that's a girl thing." Some adult males may have even have praised the sexual abuse if it was at the hands of a female by claiming, "now you're a man" or "it will make you a beast at it later."

Unfortunately, sexual abuse of boys is often hidden from the public because of the belief that it will reflect negatively on the family. Even if the perpetrator was a neighbor, coach, or close friend of the family, the sexual abuse is often not reported as often as it is when a girl is sexually abused as a child by the same individuals. The family may believe they are protecting the boy by not bringing attention to the abuse, trying to prevent negative backlash in the form of bullying and homophobic comments. Although it may seem as though they are protecting the child, by not talking about the abuse they make the boy feel as if they and the trauma they endured is not important and must be suffered in silence.

If the sexual abuse was incestuous and occurred at the hands of an aunt, uncle, cousin, sister, brother, mother, or father, there is the belief that it should be handled by the family. This may mean the family saying to not "air dirty laundry." The image of the family is placed before the needs of the boy who was sexually offended, or the sexual abuse is simply not believed. Either circumstance ostracizes the boy who was sexually abused, making them feel alone, that their emotions are not important, and stopping them from trusting members of their own family.

Stifling the voices of boys who have been sexually abused perpetuates the belief of the stoic man who is supposed to mask his emotions. Rather than being given the support of other males in their life, they are taught to remain silent, push down their emotions, continue to fight through any hardship until it is defeated, and if need be self-medicate through drugs and alcohol if the pain becomes too much to bear. It is a vicious cycle that can only be stopped by breaking the silence.

Finally, the reason you may not have disclosed your childhood sexual abuse is because you are afraid it will change the way others see you. Speaking of childhood trauma gives others a glimpse into you at your most vulnerable. It may make you feel as though others can see directly through you, exposing you completely to the world. It requires a leap of faith and trust of others that you were not prepared to have in the past. This means feeling as though you have given up the last semblance of control you have over your childhood sexual abuse. You may feel this control is all the power you have left. Although there may be fear of relinquishing this control, speaking and disclosing your sexual abuse will provide a wealth of strength that you may not have known existed.

Why You Should Break the Silence

As a male survivor of child sexual abuse, you may have felt you were the only male that this had ever happened to. This is because of the commonly held beliefs and teachings that men are the abusers and women are the abused. While this is true in some circumstances, these absolute thoughts lead to cognitive distortions that affect the way a male who has been sexually abused sees and interacts with their surroundings and others. Speaking of the sexual abuse you endured as a child lets other male survivors, and yourself, know they are not alone.

Breaking the silence means breaking the cycle of abuse. Speaking of male sexual abuse informs others who have and have not been sexually abused that this does and can occur. It also informs others that this is not uncommon. Speaking gives voice to the voiceless and provides strength where it was taken away.

Another reason to speak about your sexual abuse is to take back control over a part of your life that was taken away. Over time, as you learn to identify as a survivor, you will become proud of the man you have become. Speaking sheds light on the past and stops it from being frightening. It gives the abuse shape and substance, allowing it to be seen, addressed, and healed. Learning to disclose the sexual abuse to others takes time, practice, and guidance by a counselor or therapist. In the beginning, it will not be easy, mistakes will be made, and tears will be shed as you become the most vulnerable you have ever become, but it will become easier, and you will be stronger and better for it.

How to Disclose Your Sexual Abuse

Speaking and discussing your childhood sexual abuse with a trained counselor or therapist does not require preparation. These individuals should be trained to address and discuss sexual abuse, while allowing you to feel comfortable and safe. However, disclosing sexual abuse to others such as close friends or family does require preparation.

First, do not disclose the nature of your childhood sexual abuse until you know you are absolutely certain you are ready. While it is important to discuss the sexual abuse as a child with a spouse or partner to prepare them for possible reactions during sex, only do so when safe and comfortable. This means ensuring there is a strong foundation of support. If speaking of the sexual abuse is uncomfortable at any time, or there are feelings of extreme distress, stop, discuss those feelings and thoughts with your counselor or therapist, and continue to build a supporting foundation before continuing.

Next, when disclosing childhood sexual abuse, it is important to know that each time is different, creating different reactions from you and the person(s) you are telling. Although this is true, there are usually three different stages survivors progress through when disclosing their sexual abuse"

- **Lack of Emotion:** The sexual abuse is disclosed without emotion or feeling. Others are told as if the sexual abuse happened to someone else, or as if it were a scene in a movie.

- **Childish:** The sexual abuse is disclosed in the manner of a child who has been hurt. Others are told in order to gain sympathy and tears. It is here that the abuse is disclosed as if the survivor was reliving the abuse for the first time.

- **Truth:** The sexual abuse is disclosed as a fact, acknowledging the effects it has had on the survivor's life as a child and an adult, but knowing there was nothing that could have been done to prevent the abuse. The individual knows they are a survivor of childhood sexual abuse and identifies with that part of themselves rather than pushing it away.

Moving toward truth-telling requires practice, patience, and mistakes. In the beginning, there will be feelings of vulnerability. However, as time progresses, disclosures will become less difficult and more comfortable.

It is also important to know there are many different ways to disclose the nature of your sexual abuse. It can be expressed through art, dance, writing, or speaking. Explore what feels most comfortable, and progress through this stage with the needed support of those around you.

Below is a short story I wrote expressing the nature of sexual abuse, and it seemed my inner child had been locked away after abuse. It was first published in my book of short stories, *Thoughts in Italics* in 2007.

Action Guy (Fiction)

This is my room. I got toys! I got lots of toys! Not as many as before, but I still got toys. And they're not as new as they used to be. This one's broken, but that's okay. I still like it without the siren. I don't need a siren, as long as it still rolls. I can make the siren noise. See? *Wrrrr!* Got to put out the fire! Hurry! *Wrrrr!* See? It still works. Even without the siren. I got other toys though. I got a sailboat, a wagon and . . . Oh! Action Guy! I love Action Guy! He can do everything. Fly, *swwiisshh*, beat up bad guys, *Bang! Pow!* Burst through walls. *Boom!* And go wherever he wants by just thinking it. I wish I had that power. Just close my eyes really tight, think really hard about some place far, far away and, *poof*, I'm there. Anywhere! On a mountain, in the sky, in China, anywhere! That would be so cool. To go outside.

I used to go places like Action Guy. Run in the grass and stuff, play, but not anymore. Not with the door locked. The door is always locked, at least now. It wasn't before. Before the bad thing, Before . . . before the walls used to be blue, bright blue. And I had lots of toys. New toys with sounds, and lights, and cool, bright colors. There was carpet, and outside my windows I could see clouds and sky and grass and sun. It was fun! But now . . . now it's different since the bad thing. I'm not supposed to talk about the bad thing. It's not like it used to be since it happened. The walls are dirty and faded. The carpet is gone, and the wood is hard and cold and creaks when I walk on it. And the clouds are gone. The windows are bricked up, and I only have one tiny little hole to look out of. And I can't see anything through it. Only sun. One small dot of sun. My toys are old and no one comes to see me. I'm always the only person here. I like to play by myself, but sometimes . . . sometimes I wish I had someone else to make the siren noise and I don't always have to make believe to be happy.

No one ever let me out after the bad thing. After she made me do stuff I didn't wanna do. I didn't want to play that game anyway. She made me! She said it would be fun! It wasn't fun! It was never fun. It was scary and made me feel bad. She made me touch . . . and . . . and to get on top of her. I didn't want to. I never wanted to. But I did. So, I got in trouble. I got locked in here for being bad. It's my fault. I shouldn't have done it. Now I'm being punished. No more toys, no more clouds, or sun, or fun stuff. It's all my fault. Now I'm being punished. Now I have to wait for someone to unlock the door. They'll come. I know they will. Action Guy will come and break down the door, kick out the bricks in the windows, and then he'll grab my hand and we'll squeeze our eyes together really tight like this, and then, *poof*, we'll be outside in the sun. Flying all day and won't be my fault no more and the bad thing will be over. But . . . but the door is still locked and Action Guy hasn't come yet, so I guess . . . I guess I'll wait and play by myself. Like I always do.

Writing Exercise #4: Revealing Your Secret Identity

Depending on where you are on your journey through the healing process, you may or may not have the ability to complete this writing exercise.

Every superhero has a secret identity that they feel must be kept in order to protect not only themselves, but also those closest to them. This appeal to secrecy as a form of strength is shared by many survivors as children, and may be why they were drawn to heroes in the first place. Unfortunately, the real world is not a comic book and secrets only give strength to perpetrators and abusers. True strength comes from taking back control in the form of disclosing childhood sexual abuse and shedding light on past trauma. This creates knowledge, awareness, support, and trust where it was believed it did not exist.

If you have decided to regain this control and become strong enough to disclose the nature of your childhood sexual abuse to anyone, reflect on the experience. How did you react? How did you feel? If you have not told anyone about the nature of your sexual abuse as a child, it may be beneficial to write what you would say and to whom you would say it. Predict what you believe their reaction may be. Reflect on how you felt while writing to prepare being fully intimate and ridding yourself of the façades you believe are the only ways to survive.

Below is a full recounting of my journey throughout this stage of the healing process. The story spans over twenty years of my life and how it was not until recently I was able to tell the truth of my childhood sexual abuse as truth and identify as a survivor.

Truth Telling

The Abuse

At eight years old, I was sexually abused by my older sister. For two years I was forced to have sex with her while watching pornographic movies until it abruptly came to an end. It was either because my sister realized it was wrong or out of fear of becoming pregnant, or a combination of both. It wasn't until years later that she disclosed that she had been sexually abused when she was eight years old by her babysitter, Mr. Miller. This is not to excuse her of her actions, but to allow understanding of her attempts to cope with her childhood sexual abuse. She is now receiving treatment and we still communicate with one another.

Reaching the point where it was possible to say and write these words without an overwhelming feeling of shame and guilt did not

165

occur until twenty-five years later, three years of therapy, and full disclosure of my abuse to the members of my family.

While growing up I was afraid to even think about being raped. I wasn't even aware it was wrong until I said to a group of friends in elementary school that I had sex with my sister and they found it disgusting. Incest was not a word I had learned. Once the definition of the word was learned, I began to battle with the question about whether or not I was still a virgin. Did my abuse qualify as legitimate sex? Was it supposed to be cool or disgusting to have lost my virginity at such a young age? Was I eternally damned to hell for losing my virginity at such a young age without being married?

As these questions bounced from one to the other. I stayed to myself as much as possible, reading and writing in my journals. Even with each question about life, death, and hopeless romanticism, I dared not write about the sexual abuse out of fear that someone might read the journal and I would get in trouble.

The domestic abuse and arguments between my parents throughout high school left my mother and me homeless during my junior and senior year. We lived in the basements of cousins, uncles, and aunts. Attempting to handle this trauma pushed the sexual abuse of my childhood further from my thoughts as I attempted to battle depression, anxiety, and simply make it day to day.

Throughout these years it never crossed my mind that my sexual abuse as a child could also have been a factor in the feelings of isolation and loneliness. To fight these emotions as much as possible, extra-curricular activities and overachieving became the primary means of coping rather than disclosing my emotions or sexual abuse.

College was different than high school. The possibility of denying that I had been raped at eight years old became nearly impossible because of the introduction of sexual partners. No matter what lies my brain was able to create in order to deny my sexual abuse, my body revealed through the uncontrollable shaking after each sexual encounter with a new partner. It was here that the sexual abuse of my childhood was first disclosed to my sexual partners, of which there were not many, because I quickly learned one night stands were not an option.

However, the few there were, I cared for and felt it was my responsibility to let them know my physical reactions had nothing to do with what them, but was a result of traumatic events from the past. Although I told myself I was disclosing my sexual abuse for them, I was actually doing it for myself. I was seeking sympathy and a savior to relieve the pain I had been harboring for years. I lay in their arms, shaking and expecting all the pain and anxiety of the past to wash away with each uttered syllable. Unfortunately, each time yielded the same feelings of isolation and loneliness.

It was not until years later after the birth of my eldest daughter, Mirus, that I entered the Emergency Stage and began the process of healing. Following a year of therapy and medication, I felt I was ready to truly disclose the nature of my sexual abuse.

Telling Aunt Margaret

My wife, Sarah, had already known for years, but rather than telling my parents first, the person I told was my wife's Aunt Margaret. In my head I had rehearsed what I was going to say and how it would be said. There would be no tears. It would be explained as a matter of fact, as truth. Nothing more, nothing less.

The reason I chose Mar-Gar as the first person to tell was because she was, and still is, a person I believed I could trust and not have to explain the reasoning behind my emotions. This is a quality my wife inherited and is one of the primary reasons for falling in love with her. I also chose Margaret because I knew she would listen and not simply wait for her turn to speak. I knew she would not minimize my abuse. She would allow my vulnerability, and I trusted her with it.

From there I told my family, beginning with my sister. Although she was the abuser, she deserved to know that others in the family would know about an incident that affected her as well. Rather than make a phone call I was unsure I could handle, and because we had stopped talking when I had begun therapy, I sent a text message letting her know I was going to tell the family about what had happened between us as kids. I also invited her to a therapy session, but she was not ready to begin her journey toward healing.

Telling Daniel

Next, was my brother, Daniel. Throughout my year of therapy, and struggling through my Emergency Stage, he had been my primary cheerleader, and he still was after the disclosure of the sexual abuse. Afterward, he felt he was partly to blame for the abuse because of the conflicts between him and my father that led to him leaving the house and joining the military. I assured him there was nothing he could have done and that he was the only one who had nothing to be held accountable for.

Telling My Mother

Then I told my mother, and I knew she would be the most difficult to tell. Although I would have preferred to tell her in person, I could not because of the distance between Peoria, Illinois, and Baltimore, Maryland, so I called her on the phone.

The conversation began with reassurance to her that I was fine and getting help, but that she should know I had been raped by my sister (her daughter) for two years, beginning when I was eight years old. She said very little, apologized, and seemed to get off the phone relatively quickly. At the time I felt a little hurt that she didn't say more, but months later she explained that she had felt shocked and ashamed that this had happened in her house and she had no idea. The other reason for her silence was because my sister had already told her about the sexual abuse years before, but was told that it had only happened once. The truth of what had actually happened left her reeling. In order to help us both heal from this trauma, she came to Baltimore, attended a book signing and discussion of my book, *Raped Black Male*, came to a joint therapy session to understand why the abuse happened, and sincerely apologized for this ever happening to me. Over the years she has continued to remain supportive.

Telling My Father

Finally, I told my father. This was a conversation I did not know how to prepare for, so I began in the same way I had with my mother. I reassured him that I was okay, but that for two years I had been raped by my sister (his daughter). Although the conversation began in the same way, it ended much differently. After explaining the sexual abuse he said to me, "Forget about it. It's in the past. The best thing you can do is move on." To say I was shocked at the time would be an understatement. However, I found that I was not only shocked, but angry as well. Rather than cower and continue to harbor the secret I had been carrying for over twenty years, I responded with defiance and honesty. I told him that I couldn't forget. The abuse was something I had to live with every day and that it could not be forgotten. He apologized, hung up, and did not speak with me for nine months. It wasn't until after Daniel told him that he needed to start talking to me that my father proceeded to text and talk with me as if nothing had happened. The illusion of normalcy was not something I could return to, so I asked my father for a written letter apologizing for abandoning me after I told him about the sexual abuse. Rather than comply, he responded back via text. He said:

> Okay, son. I will respect your request. You are a grown man and able to make your own decisions. I'm glad you are doing better and I'm really sorry to hear about Sarah's brother. Let me say this ... I love my kids the same. You, Daniel, and Tarana are my life. I don't love one no more or less than the other one. If I could take your hurt I would. I can't so I can do only what I am able to do. But remember this. We can only start healing after we forgive. If I could change things I would. I'm sure your sister is hurting. I'm sure she had no intention of hurting you. Then or now. She has to live with the fact of what she did and face everyone who read your book and label her a rapist. This has to be really hard for her. I'm sure this has been really hard on you. I can only imagine how hard it has been. I know my kid and know you

are strong. You can and will overcome this. It's in the blood. No matter what you think, this too will pass. If you need me I will always be there for you. Don't be a stranger. I don't want you to one day think I missed out on a lot of my family's life. She, Daniel, Tina and me are your family. Love you unconditionally. Da.

It's taken a long time to digest these words and understand them. The message does a number of things. First, it minimized my sexual abuse and sympathizes with the abuser rather than the victim. When he said, "She has to live with the fact of what she did and face everyone who read your book and label her a rapist." This reveals a need to not "air dirty laundry" and hold people accountable for their actions by using the correct language to describe their behavior. A person who forces an individual to have sex against their will is a rapist. There is no doubt the word causes pain to the individual being labeled as such, but there is no other word to describe those actions. It is regrettable to have to use this word in reference to my sister, but to do otherwise would be to not hold the abuser accountable, but it also fails to attempt to stop the cycle of sexual abuse.

Second, the message reveals my father's refusal to take responsibility for his failure as a parent to protect his children. Although he says, "If I could take your hurt I would," this statement, and others, does not reveal his knowledge or acceptance of his role in allowing this to happen. A parent's responsibility is to protect their children. To not do so does not mean the parent has failed because there is no such thing as the perfect parent. Mistakes will be made. However, following those mistakes, parents must admit their shortcomings to let their children know what happened was not the child's fault and for the parent to apply what they have learned to future situations. Unfortunately, my father does not accept any accountability and so places the blame on the shoulders of others.

Third, it reveals the mentality of many men, especially black men, who came of age before and during the Civil Rights Movement.

My father makes statements such as, "I know my kid and I know you are strong," and "It's in the blood." These statements are similar to Green Lantern's when he found out Roy had been doing drugs. Green Lantern explained how he had taught Roy to "hang tough." My father's words are similar because it reveals a need to teach boys to remain silent, not feel, deny the pain, and move on from life's hardships. However, for older black men this is especially true because during the Civil Rights Movement and the era of Jim Crow, denial of pain, hardship, and abuse was the only way to survive. It was their coping mechanism to handle physical abuse and the mental trauma of not being able to keep their family safe. Denying having been hurt could have prevented men like my father from being lynched and killed as he grew up in rural Mississippi. Denial and forgetting were the only coping strategies fathers could pass on to their sons when basic human rights had been stripped away. This means that when their sons, nephews, and cousins suffered a traumatic episode, such as childhood sexual abuse, they teach and reinforce the only way of life they have ever known by forgetting it ever happened and burying the emotions that accompany trauma. This is not a justification for his message to my sexual abuse, but provides context in my understanding of why he said it. As a male survivor, it means no longer viewing myself as a victim, understanding the wrongs of the past, learning from them, and moving forward.

Telling Other Family Members, Friends, and Co-Workers

Following the disclosure of my childhood sexual abuse to my immediate family I told my in-laws, friends, extended family, and some co-workers. With each disclosure I felt empowered and wanted to help male survivors like myself. It's for this reason I wrote *Raped Black Male*. At the time my therapist, Susan, advised against it. Not to hide my sexual abuse, but because I was still moving along the healing process and she did not want me to have any setbacks. Against her better judgment, I published anyway, thinking it was my responsibility to use my writing to let other male survivors know they were not alone. Unfortunately I was not prepared for the backlash.

Repercussions

With the publication of *Raped Black Male*, I did not expect my immediate family to approve. Although it was not received with open arms because of its exposure of family secrets, overall it has been viewed as a good thing. My in-laws and friends praised its honestly, bravery, and insight into the life of a male survivor. Other male, as well as female, survivors found it helpful as well. Unfortunately, the largest amount of push-back I received was from the principal of my school.

As a teacher of English in Baltimore City, I always inform my students of my previous published books and any new projects I am working on. This helps them understand the writing process and that their teacher uses the skills he teaches in the classroom as a published author. When *Raped Black Male* was released, my response and explanation to my students was no different than my previous four publications. I let them know about the book, informed them of the next book I was writing, and included the new title in my classroom library. Before doing so, I informed the parents of my students about the memoir at back-to-school night, along with my restrictions for after-school help because of obligations with therapy appointments, and how the memoir would be included in my library. After doing so, no parents raised any concerns to me or other administration. Instead, many admired my courage and honesty in keeping them informed. However, when the students in my classes began to read the memoir, walking around the school carrying a book entitled *Raped Black Male,* I was quickly called into the principal's office.

Once in the office of my principal, I was told that students would need to have permission slips to read my book because of possible parental complaints, some of the book's content, and the difficult vocabulary of the text would make it difficult for the students to comprehend its meaning. I was told that, until students provided permission slips, all the books had to be confiscated. I agreed with her reasoning and I still do. Providing a permission slip to read a novel that involves a sensitive topic such as sexual abuse protects the school and me as an educator. However, before leaving I was also told to not only collect the books, but that I was no longer allowed to state that I was a survivor of child sexual abuse. Her exact words were to "Let it lie." After she said it, I wasn't sure if I understood what she was telling me to do. Was she telling me to no longer tell my students I was a survivor of sexual abuse, or to never mention it while at school whether it was to students, parents, or other staff members? Confused, I simply said okay and left the office.

Immediately the copies of *Raped Black Male* were collected from the students, as I tried to make sense of what I was feeling. After reporting the conversation to my therapist, Susan, she immediately told me, without hesitation, to quit. I was shocked that she would tell me to do something so drastic when she knows how much I hate spontaneity. Having order and a plan while remaining hypervigilance and a workaholic are the primary coping mechanisms I have worked to overcome. This was not the response I was expecting. When I asked why she wanted me to quit my job, half believing she was joking, she explained how my principal's response was going to wreak havoc on my psyche, causing my journey through healing to relapse. At the time I didn't believe her. Like all other difficult situations in my life, I believed that, like Superman, I could handle anything life threw my way. But over a series of months I began to see that Susan was right. Without warning, I suddenly became more depressed. Thoughts of suicide and feelings of anxiety never left my mind. The stress of no longer feeling safe in the place I worked caused physical sickness, which resulted in hospitalization and being out of the classroom for over a month as my body fought to recover a viral heart infection. I did not understand the reason why the conversation was so devastating then, but I do now.

When my principal, an older white female, told me to no longer say I was a survivor of childhood sexual abuse, it had the same psychological effect as being reoffended. When she told me to "let it lie" and no longer identify as a survivor and remain silent about my abuse in the same way my sister had told me to "not tell anyone," she had taken the role of my sister as the abuser, and the control I was beginning to gain over my life by disclosing my sexual abuse was gone. The same way I was told to remain silent about my abuse in the past was happening by the leader of a different organization that she and other staff and faculty called a family.

Being told to no longer identify as a survivor of childhood sexual abuse was the same, and had the same effect, as telling an individual who identifies as homosexual that they could no longer state they are gay; a Latino to no longer express their heritage and culture through their accent, clothes, food, and way of life; that a Jewish man could no longer identify with his religion by wearing a yamaka; or that a Muslim woman could no longer identify with her faith by wearing a hijab. Each is a part of the identity of the individual in the same way being a survivor is a part of mine. In the statement my principal made to not say I was a survivor, made the sexual abuse I endured at eight years old a choice by me rather than rape by another.

Following the conversation, I began to notice signs, and feel as though I was being ostracized by my principal. I also became increasingly afraid of doing my job correctly without being reprimanded. The full impact of the statement, "let it lie," was not felt until I filed for a personal day to attend a different Baltimore City Public School to discuss my book and male childhood sexual abuse to students who had read my memoir and the novel *Speak* by Laurie Halse Anderson, which explores a unit on rape culture in American society. While speaking, I received a text from my principal that I needed to inform her when I was going to be absent, even if I filled out all the proper paperwork beforehand. It was then that I told my principal about my fear, and that I would like to have a meeting to relieve my growing fear of being in an unsafe work environment. She agreed.

At the time it was my hope that the way I had been feeling and the thoughts I had been having were all a simple misunderstanding that could be cleared up with a simple conversation about how I was feeling and what both of us could do to mend the situation. It was not. When my principal entered the room, sat down, and began the meeting with no amount of compassion or concern in her voice or on her face, I knew my thoughts had not been imagined. Below is a transcript of the conversation recorded by the vice-principal during the meeting.

Here are the notes from our meeting today.

Time: 2:05

Attendees: Principal, Kenny Rogers, Vice Principal

Our meeting began with Principal giving the floor to Kenny to address his concerns. Kenny identified a number of issues he had with Principal.

After meeting in the fall, Principal asked Kenny to not allow students to read his memoir without parental consent. She also asked him to "let it lie," which sat with him for "a long time in the wrong way."

When Kenny called out when his brother-in-law passed, Kenny stated that Principal told him his calling out was a burden on the team.

After TJ passed, Kenny was hurt that Principal did not give him a condolence card. As his advisory partner, he expected that from her.

When Kenny called out due to suicidal thoughts, Principal didn't say anything to him about it the next day. He felt that she was being cold.

When Principal spoke to him about the letters about hoodies, he took exception to Principal not celebrating his Donors' Choose project. He thought she would be pleased that he was trying to get $1,600 in new books. Also, the middle school's athletic shirts are produced at his family's printing company. He didn't believe that wasn't appropriate.

When Principal removed herself from being his advisory partner, Kenny was upset that it happened so abruptly and that she didn't give him a heads up.

Patterson invited him to speak at their school because they are doing a full unit on rape culture. Because of the things listed above, he was scared to tell Principal because he doesn't believe he can be open or talk to her about abuse. He also felt that Principal shouldn't have texted him about his absence because the notes stated that he would be out.

Because of these things, his therapist has advised him to quit.

After Kenny identified his issues, she asked him to explain why he was afraid of her. Principal said that she could understand why he was hurt but not why he was fearful.

Kenny clarified his statement by saying that he was raped and abused by an older woman in his family. Because the middle school is a family and Principal is the head of the family who doesn't show him love, in his "messed up mind," he equates that to doing something wrong. He also explained to Principal that he lives in constant fear every day.

Principal apologized to Kenny for not being supportive toward him during that time. She was dealing with her own trauma. She explained that she stepped away from being his advisory partner because she didn't feel that she was being a good leader or a good partner. She stated that she heard him and she respected his feelings deeply.

Principal went on to explain that at the end of the day, she's his supervisor. It is her job to make sure that teachers fulfill their role, which is to teach the curriculum, teach it well, and make sure that students are safe and supported. She was glad that he remembered that she didn't silence him but just asked him to have parental consent. She went on to say that she wants to make sure that his "emotional history isn't imposed on students. We can't use classroom as a therapeutic outlet, whether it's rape, divorce, or illness. Even if it connects, we can't hold our students to that captive audience without their consent or granting them permission to leave, if they choose." She continued to explain that she's not comfortable with Kenny declaring his abuse to students on day 1 because it's not the time. She also told Kenny that she respects the therapist, their relationship, and the question about whether being at the middle school is a place for him.

Principal explained that she has to answer to North Avenue and families. Because of this, it's important to be mindful of the gray area particularly when dealing with 12 year olds. She told Kenny that she respects his journey, process, and healing, but the biggest concern was the timing in class. She has no problem with him sharing his story with a club or a group. Kenny nodded his head no.

She also told Kenny that as his supervisor they must communicate. She told him that they will have a third party when they communicate privately. She also reminded him that when he calls out, at the middle school, we give a call or a text as a heads up. Lastly, she told Kenny that it was not her intention to focus on him or target him. She acknowledges Kenny's feelings of hurt regarding his perceived lack of love and support. She apologized for hurting him and being distracted.

She asked Kenny, "Knowing the expectation, is this a place you want to be?"

Kenny responded by saying, "I love to teach and I love the job but I don't know essentially, if I'm not allowed to be me."

Principal replied, "I want you to be judicious in what you share to 12 year olds."

Kenny explained that his experiences let his students know that he is human and that his past shapes him. Because of his vulnerability, he was able to get help for a student who was being abused at home. When he tells his students his stories about his hardships, he feels like those are things that he has to share. He wants to be an example to his students that they can overcome hardships. Students should know he's not from privilege.

Principal points out that when he introduced the syllabus for the year on day one, he gave his name and let them know that he is a rape survivor. She told him that she understood that relationships happen but she wants him to walk the fine line with students. She doesn't accept the notion that she has taken the role of his abuser, and she doesn't believe that she's asking him to do anything that is inappropriate.

Kenny told Principal that she can't tell him how to think.

Principal agreed with him in saying that she was unsure about him becoming comfortable with her at the middle school. She would respect his desire to work with someone else and wondered if high school would be a better fit given Patterson's interest in his work.

She repeated her expectations. They are:

To send a courtesy text when calling out and let him know that the message could be sent to Vice Principal.

She apologized for not being more warm.

To communicate more about things that affect the middle school. Admin should know so they are aware, not caught off guard and to allow room to highlight good things.

Kenny doubled checked to make sure his Donors Choose project was okay, because he didn't get a response.

Principal added that she felt the coldness that Kenny spoke of, and it can happen in two ways: on her end but also his. The disconnect is obvious to her, and she will reflect on it.

She also requested to be updated on his future plans regarding the middle school.

End.

After the meeting, I felt lost. I wanted to quit. A formal complaint was filed through Baltimore Teachers Union, but I was told there was nothing I could do except change schools without losing my teaching certification for not fulfilling my teaching contract.

Over the next months of the school year, I became severely depressed and physically ill from new medications to relieve feelings of anxiety and depression. I shed ten pounds from consistent vomiting and was a diagnosed by my a cardiologist as contracting a viral heart infection called pericarditis, keeping me from work for over a month as my body fought the infection and my heart healed.

It's been many months since that conversation. I've spent hours replaying each word in my mind while lying in bed unable to move because of the pain in my chest. Weeks were spent wasting energy and attempting to understand what I had done to be treated so poorly. Eventually I arrived at a place of peace after being able to equate my experience with an episode of *My Little Pony*. I know this may sound weird, but stay with me. As a father of two toddler girls, I have watched a lot of the new episodes of *My Little Pony*. Sarah makes fun of me and says that I have defiantly become a *brony* (a fan of *My Little Pony*), which I have no problem in stating is true. The only other adult male I know who may love the show as much as I do . . . or more, is Patten Oswald.

In my infinite wisdom of Equestria (the magical land of *My Little Pony*) and how friendship is magic, much of the interaction I had with my principal (and many others throughout my life) reminds me of Pinky Pie and the first time she met Cranky Doodle Donkey.

In season two, episode eighteen of *My Little Pony*, "A Friend in Deed," Pinky Pie meets somepony who will not accept her friendship. Pinky Pie is a pony who is the life of the party. She strives to make everypony happy, laugh, feel comfortable, and enjoy themselves fully. So, when she meets a donkey that is sad and refuses to accept her friendship, Pinky goes out of her way to make him happy and find out why he won't accept her friendship. No matter how many times he yells and tells her to mind her own business, Pinky Pie refuses to give up turning him into a friend. After continued prodding, eventually she discovers the reason Cranky Doodle is so miserable is because he lost the love of his life when he was young and has spent his entire life searching to find her. Because Pinky knows and is friends with everyone, she is able to use her connections to find the donkey's long lost love, transforming Cranky Doodle from an acquaintance to a friend, and everypony (and donkey) lives happily-ever-after.

At the end of the episode, I remember thinking to myself, "That plot is ridiculous!" The absurdity of the plot was not because of the talking ponies and donkeys, but because it sent the wrong message to children. It taught children that if you try hard enough and never give up, you can please and be friends with everyone. It also taught them that with enough love they can make someone love them in return. It's the same lesson taught in many Disney classic films such as *Beauty and the Beast*. Films and television shows such as these express a belief that one person's love can fix another person's life, transforming their mediocre acquaintance into a strong, viable, loving relationship. This simply is not true.

Understand, I do believe love trumps hate and that the world needs peace and understanding now more than ever, but no matter what an individual may try, or how much they may want another person's love, sometimes receiving this love may be an impossibility. A broken individual cannot simply be fixed with the love of someone else. Healing and transformation only occurs when an individual wants to make a change in their own life. Everyone cannot be pleased. Everyone cannot be friends. However, they can be cordial, kind, pleasant, and understanding of another person's feelings and experiences. Learning and accepting this lesson has taken my entire life thus far.

The negative interactions I had with my principal concerning my sexual abuse as a child was the first instance in my life when another individual genuinely did not like me and there was no amount of wasted energy I could exert to change this fact. Throughout the three-year professional relationship I had with my principal, I attempted to be kind, relate, and move from a perceived position of threat to one of friendship, but it did not work. However, this feeling of not being accepted and liked by my supervisor was a personal issue I had to deal with on my own. At the time, I believed changing these feelings I had was the responsibility of my principal when it wasn't. These are my views and my feelings, so transferring these negative thoughts and feelings onto my principal was a cognitive distortion and automatic thought I had to transform. It means eliminating the view of myself and my actions as those of a superhero. I am not Superman. I am only human and so is she. I have to practice what I preach and eliminate forms of hatred and biases that I may carry and remain understanding of another's thoughts and feelings. I do not have to accept them, but I do have to allow others to have them.

Looking back over the span of my healing process, I now see that my principal was also dealing with some very challenging and life-threatening personal issues. Unfortunately, attempting to manage professional responsibilities with personal challenges was difficult to manage and meant an absence of sound judgment, and acceptance of the emotions of others was thrown out the window. Am I condoning her actions? Not at all. However, in the same way I recognized the cognitive distortions of my father, I recognize my principal's as well. Was I completely innocent in the interactions with my principal? Yes and no. As a survivor, my rights were violated. However, as an individual, I cannot make or expect everyone to hold the same views as I do. It is wrong, and in the end it means whitewashing the identity of someone else. Being human means being an individual with individual thoughts, beliefs, hopes, and fears while not imposing or limiting the views of others. Everyone may not share this belief, but it's part of my hero code.

I do not know why my principal told me to no longer identify as a survivor of childhood sexual abuse. I know many individuals who have been sexually abused in their lifetime and who have yet to fully heal from their own trauma, attempt to control the actions and thoughts of others through hypervigilance in order to retain some semblance of the power that was taken. I also know that, through all of my disclosures, it became easier and helpful to me and others rather than remaining silent. Speaking has taught me about people, trust, and that silence is not an option.

Chapter Seventeen
Understanding It Wasn't Your Fault

A hero is born among a hundred, a wise man is found among a thousand, but an accomplished one might not be found even among a hundred thousand men.

—Plato

Cognitive Distortions

This stage of the healing process may be the longest and most difficult for a male survivor of childhood sexual abuse, for a number of reasons. One primary reason is because you are a male and you may have been convinced that males cannot be raped. Depending on the nature of the sexual abuse, some thoughts you may have include, "If I did not want to have sex, then why did I have an erection?" or "Why did some parts of the sexual abuse feel good?"

No matter the sexual abuse, there is no way to control the body from certain stimulations. Just because you were in a sexually abusive situation, that does not place blame on your shoulders as the victim. One of the ways to come to this understanding is to explore the cognitive distortions in your own thoughts that led to the belief that it was your fault and that if you truly wanted to prevent the sexual abuse you could have. The ten cognitive distortions you could have are:

1. **All-or-Nothing Thinking:** Things are viewed in absolute black-and-white categories. This means there can only be a right and wrong answer, with no gray area in-between. These thoughts lead some survivors to view themselves as being either a hero or a villain. To grow and heal, survivors must move beyond all-or-nothing thinking and examine

situations completely to understand the full effects of the thoughts. Examples of these thoughts are, "Men cannot be raped" and "It was my fault because I was the boy." This reveals there is only one correct answer that eventually leads to survivors believing it was their fault.

2. **Overgeneralizations:** A negative event is viewed as a never-ending pattern of defeat. This means survivors view actions and themselves through the lens of a victim rather than a survivor. The survivor believes the world is always against them and there is no way to win. So why try? This sense of isolation and defeatism only leads to shame that the survivor could not prevent the sexual abuse.

3. **Mental Filters:** The survivor dwells on negatives rather than positives. Some thoughts during this cognitive distortion may be "What's the point? Even if I try I'll still fail" or "It's better to not get my hopes up so I won't be disappointed later." Viewing only the negative will lead to negative thoughts of themselves as the cause of their downfall, rather than their rise and eventual success.

4. **Discounting the Positives:** The survivor insists that their accomplishments or positive qualities don't count. This means that the survivor never views the positive in their actions. Rather, the good things are because of the actions of others. This distortion ensures they always view themselves as the villain, unable to win, providing a small amount of power in believing they can control their own fate.

5. **Jumping to Conclusions:**

   a. **Mind reading:** The survivor assumes people are acting negatively without definite evidence. Some common thoughts may be "Because of the way they said it, I knew they were mad at me," or "I could tell by the way they were standing they were annoyed," or "It's not what they said, but what they didn't say." While mind reading may have been useful as a child to anticipate when future abuses would take place, as an adult it only provides wasted energy in trying to please everyone, in an effort to not feel ashamed or at fault for the sexual abuse.

b. **Fortune Telling:** The survivor arbitrarily believes circumstances will turn out badly. Without justification or warrant, they assume the worse. This is done to limit their amount of hope, because as a child, hope was a luxury that they could not afford if it meant surviving. Fortune-telling allows survivors to anticipate the worse and remain hypervigilant to protect themselves from the chaos and loss of control that was a product of their sexual abuse.

6. **Magnification or Minimization:** The survivor blows situations way out of proportion or shrinks their importance. This means placing value in the wrong place. While the emotions of a survivor may be minimized, the importance of others may be inflated. In some instances, this allows attention to be taken away from the survivor, allowing them to remain unnoticed and protected through invisibility. In other circumstances, it means continuing to identify as the victim to create chaos in the lives of others to maintain a sense of control.

7. **Emotional Reasoning:** The survivor reasons with how they feel. This means believing that if they feel a certain way then that must be what they are. For example, they may say to themselves, "I feel worthless, so I must be worthless." This distortion allows continued feelings of doubt and worthlessness, while allowing a limited sense of control through false prophecies destined to come true.

8. **"Should" or "Shouldn't Have" Statements:** The survivor criticizes themselves and their actions through "should," "ought." "must," and "have to." This distortion puts unwarranted stress on the survivor in beliefs of what they

must, should, or shouldn't have done. It allows the survivor to abuse themselves verbally, saying things in their mind they would never say to their worst enemy, while reaffirming the beliefs of their abuser that they are worthless and the abuse was their fault.

9. **Labeling:** Instead of stating, "I made a mistake," the survivor calls themselves names such as "stupid" or "idiot." Stating these words dehumanizes their actions and helps to reaffirm the way the abuser made them feel through the sexual abuse. These thoughts force the survivor to view themselves as less and the abuse as their own doing.

10. **Personalization and Blame:** The survivor blames themselves for something they weren't entirely responsible for, or they blame themselves while denying their role in the problem. In either circumstance, it means playing the victim. It ensures a semblance of control through a false belief of control and accountability that was never their own, or righteousness in the false belief that they are completely innocent of all wrongdoing because of the sexual abuse endured in the past that resulted in the victimization of the present.

To overcome the belief that the sexual abuse of your childhood was your fault, you must recognize and change the cognitive distortions so that you no longer play the role of the victim and see truth in the actions of others and yourself. It takes practice and effort, but can be accomplished through useful exercises. To help with this process, use the writing exercise below.

Writing Exercise #5: Changing Your Thoughts

To help you understand the cognitive distortions you incur daily as a survivor, there is an exercise that can help lead you toward changing your thoughts in a positive way. It is called a cost-benefit analysis.

To complete this activity, it is recommended that you talk through the results with your counselor or therapist to ensure the correct conclusions are reached. First, write the thought you believe needs to be corrected, and then coincide with one or more of the listed cognitive distortions. For example, "What I did wasn't perfect, therefore I am worthless."

Next, read through the list of cognitive distortions that match the distorted thoughts. Some cognitive distortions that match the thought above are: all-or-nothing, overgeneralizations, mental filters, discounting the positives, minimization, emotional reasoning, labeling, personalization, and blame. Take the time to analyze why each distortion matches your thoughts.

Finally, change the thought to rid it of the cognitive distortions. This is the most difficult and requires the most practice. Changing the thought above to rid it of the cognitive distortions would be "I did my best." It is simple, but truthful and to the point.

Take the time and remain patient as you change the way you think. Over time, the process will become easier and the way you view yourself and your actions will change.

Cognitive Distortion Exercise: Changing Your Thoughts		
Distorted Thought	*Cognitive Distortions*	*New Thought*
What I did wasn't perfect, therefore I am worthless.	all-or-nothing, overgeneralizations, mental filters, discounting the positives, minimization, emotional reasoning, labeling, personalization, and blame	I did my best and that's good enough.

Writing Exercise #6: Child, Parent, Adult Thinking

Although identifying the cognitive distortions in your thoughts is beneficial, it is difficult and time consuming. A simple strategy to help change distorted automatic thoughts can be to label and change them from the thoughts of a child or parent to that of an adult.

- **Childish Thoughts:** These thoughts are filled with excuses and passing of blame to others. For example, "I didn't do anything wrong because it wasn't my responsibility" or "Bad things are always happening to me and not to anyone else." Rather than explore your role in the possible problem, your actions are justified and looked down on by others, when you believe they should be praised.

- **Parental Thoughts:** These thoughts are filled with "should" and "must" statements, making the survivor believe they have no choice. Examples are: "I didn't do anything to deserve attention" or "I have to follow the rules."

- **Adult Thoughts:** The goal of this exercise is to reframe the automatic thoughts so that they are no longer those of an uncompromising parent or a child controlled by their needs and wants. For example, "I *do* the best I can." Changing these automatic thoughts to resemble those of an adult takes practice and help.

In this writing exercise, work with your therapist, counselor, or support system to identify your automatic thoughts that are those of a child or parent, and how to reframe them to those of an adult. To help with this process, use the graphic organizer below.

Automatic Thought Exercise				
Automatic Thought	Childish Reasoning	Parental Reasoning	Cognitive Distortions	Adult Thought
Bad things are always happening to me and no one else.	X		overgeneralizations, mental filters, discounting the positives, labeling	I do the best I can.

The Child Within

The boy/young man who was sexually abused as a child is hidden and locked away. In order to survive, the male may have had to lock that child away and become what they believed to be a real man. This meant locking away the need to have emotions or trust in others in the same trusting manner as other children. Because of the child sexual abuse, it may be difficult for a survivor to even remember being a child. Portions of their childhood may be a blank slate, creating the belief that they were never a child or that they have always been the stoic male who seemed to carry the weight of the world on his shoulders. This is not true.

The falsehood of the belief may not become fully aware until the birth of a child, or when a child in the care of a survivor reaches the age in which the survivor was sexually abused. When this happens, the survivor may find themselves becoming a villain rather than a hero as they experience moments of rage and anxiety without warning, in the same way as Joseph Kerr as he fought to keep the chaos of the Joker at bay as described in the villains portion of this book. The only cure is to make contact with the little boy inside and make peace with him.

Male survivors may often find themselves saying to their inner child, "Stop being so weak! You can push harder than that! You still have more you can give and do if you stop holding back!" These statements are abusive to the inner child and continue the thought of having little to no self-worth. Altering the cognitive distortions and reframing automatic thoughts to those of an adult will create better mental health and long-term, lasting happiness.

Altering these thoughts cannot be accomplished overnight, but the abuse of the inner child must be recognized. When harsh words are being directed at the inner child, change the words to those of praise and encouragement. Make peace in the knowledge that the very best is being done and that nothing more can be asked. When this understanding is reached, the inner child will no longer be viewed as the bad guy but a person deserving of love and support the same as anyone else. It is then you will truly know the sexual abuse was in no way your fault and that you did not have the strength to stop it then, but you are strong now.

Writing Exercise #7: A Letter to the Past

Write a letter to the little boy who was abused as a child. Tell him the good things he has to offer the world. Provide encouragement that the future will get better. Say the things you wish would have been said by your parents or family when you were young and life seemed impossible to bear.

My Letter

Hey Kenny,

What's up? This is me from the future. That's right, your future self is talking to you from the year 2017. Crazy, right? I know you have a lot of questions, but here is what you really want to know. No, there are no hover boards, flying cars, or jetpacks. That's the bad news. The good news is that you made it to thirty-two years old with most of your hair. I know, thirty-two! I'm old, but it's not that bad. In fact, you own your own house, you're married, and you have two daughters.

Stop freaking out! It's not bad at all! It's great! All three of them are beautiful and amazing.

I don't want to give away the details of how you end up all the way in Baltimore, Maryland, from Peoria, Illinois, but I wanted to let you know that you made it.

Look, I know things are hard right now, with everything happening with Daniel and Daddy, the arguments between Mommy and Daddy, and that thing with T you think you can't talk about; it all feels like two much. You feel alone and all you really want to do is curl up with a book and disappear, or start running and never stop. You feel like you're nothing, but you're wrong.

You're amazing!

It's who you are now that makes me who I am. Your imagination, love of learning, and reading fantasy and science fiction is what makes me an author, awesome teacher, and loving father.

Right now, you're scared. Fear of the unknown is around every corner. You feel like you don't have the courage or intelligence to face the future, but you do. Know and believe when I say it gets better and easier. The friends and new family you create will be better than you could ever imagine. They will support you. They will love you and you will love them. Throughout each stage of your life, you will impact and change the lives of people around you for the better.

Times will become difficult, and doubts will race throughout all parts of your mind about the man you will become. You will question the future and whether or not you are moving in the right direction. If you hold on to the belief that tomorrow will be better than today, if you do your best to be your best self, then everything will be okay.

I know you don't hear this often. because it is rarely said, but I love you. You are an amazing, awesome human being whose greatest strengths are the kindness he shares with others and the consistent striving to be better. Don't worry about the negativity of others—even if it comes from the family who was supposed to love and protect you.

You're a good man, Charlie Brown. Know it and own it.

Later days,

Future Kenny

Emotions

As a male survivor, you may have come to fear your emotions. This may be because emotions were a source of pain in an already traumatic world, and may have had limiting access to any and all of your emotions. While this coping strategy may have allowed you to survive the trauma of your sexual abuse as a child, as an adult it limits your interactions and strength of valuable relationships with people you love.

One emotion you may be afraid to express is anger, because of fear of what it may lead to. Pushing this emotion away more than all the others may have been because of the belief that it protected you and those closest to you, in the same way a superhero puts the needs and wants of others before themselves. However, anger, along with an expression of all the other emotions, is beneficial and crucial to healing.

While there will be moments in which you feel numb to all emotions, take the time to examine your emotions using an emotion chart. Do this activity with your therapist or counselor when it seems you are lost in a whirlwind of feelings or numb to them all. And while you may fear expressing your anger, it is healthy and critical to have this anger toward the abuser and those who did not protect you as a child when you were their responsibility. Without admitting this anger, you will never be able to reach a resolution and move on.

Although anger is normal and healthy, it is important to understand healthy and unhealthy ways of expressing anger. Use this guide to help understand how to express and relieve anger constructively:

- Do not hurt yourself or anyone else
- Do not destroy property unless it is owned by you and designated as being able to be destroyed
- Do not imagine hurting yourself
- You can scream
- You can punch a pillow or punching bag
- You can write a letter and burn it
- You can run
- You can do other exercises

Grieving

Barry Allen grieved the loss of his mother when she was murdered when he was boy years into adulthood, but never fully accepted her death. Instead, he devoted his life to putting away criminals and preventing others from having to endure the same loss. However, because Barry never fully grieved the loss of his mother, he ended up becoming the villain of his own story in the graphic novel *Flashpoint*. By traveling into the future, Barry stopped his mother's murder, but altered all of reality. In the end, to set things right, Barry had to grieve and accept the fact that certain parts of his life had been taken away, and would never be the same no matter how hard he tried, when his mother was murdered. As a male survivor, you do not need the ability to run faster than the speed of light and travel into the past to prevent your sexual abuse, but you do have the ability to grieve and mourn the effects of your sexual abuse on your life.

While anger is an important emotion to express, to move forward throughout the healing process it is also vital to grieve and mourn the things that were lost or taken away when the sexual abuse occurred. This means feeling more than sadness over this horrific event, but knowing and expressing sorrow over the lasting effects of the sexual abuse.

As a survivor of child sexual abuse there may be experiences you will never have. Experiences such as having and giving your virginity to someone you care for, or knowing what it means to grow up in a stable home. Questions concerning the direction of your life and the people you loved will arise as you move throughout the process of healing, causing you to mourn the life and happiness you could have had.

Unfortunately, these parts of your life and the answers to these questions can never be answered. While this is a fact that cannot be altered, the pain of its truth is tangible, real, and must be acknowledged. This grieving can happen numerous times throughout your journey as more memories surface and the truth of your sexual abuse becomes revealed. Do not rush the grieving process. Let it walk in tandem with the anger you have, to allow it the ability and time to be fully understood and mended.

Writing Exercise #8: What If . . .

Following your sexual abuse, you may have developed questions as an adult about who you could have been or what you could have done. These questions will cause you to mourn the life and experiences you lost and that were taken. For this writing exercise, write those questions you may have exploring the possibility of the life you would have had without being sexually abused. After writing these questions, list and explain the things you have to mourn the loss of. This list can and should be added to as you move throughout the healing process.

This is not a race. Write, rest, then return to reflect and add.

Below are my questions and what I have to mourn:

Questions

If I wasn't sexually, abused by a black woman would I still have married and fallen in love with Sarah?

If I hadn't developed a fear of the future and life being stripped away without remaining hypervigilant, would I have had the courage to pursue a career as a professional actor?

If I wasn't sexually abused, would I have developed a love for reading and writing?

Did I rip apart my family by talking about my sexual abuse?

Should I have just kept my mouth shut about my sexual abuse?

How can I have been sexually abused by my sister and still love her as my sister?

Mourn the Loss of Childhood: I must mourn the fact that my childhood was not normal. This comes with some sense of anger for those who had a stable home and will never know the trauma of domestic violence and sexual abuse.

Mourn the Loss of Courage: Fear of the unknown and venturing down the unstable path has always held me back. I have to grieve the life I could have lived without a fear of spontaneity after control of my life was stripped away after the sexual abuse.

Mourn the Loss of Family and Friends: The sexual abuse of the past will always make me feel alone and isolated from others. No matter how much work I do, I will never feel as though those closest to me truly know how I feel. I must mourn the sense of inclusion I will never have.

Chapter Eighteen
Spirituality and Forgiveness

It wasn't until we got over the self-pity that we were able to accept suffering as a part of our life with Christ. A man or woman reaches this plane only when he or she ceases to be the hero.

—Corazon Aquino

Forgiveness Is Not Required

This stage of the healing process does not have to be experienced by every survivor in order to completely heal. Coming to terms with religious and spiritual beliefs is a task that must be accomplished completely independent of the survivor, without the help of a therapist or counselor. This is not because they would not like to help, but because they cannot. Spirituality must be reached with the heart, not the brain. It requires a leap of faith. This means moving toward finding forgiveness independently.

When many individuals hear the word *forgiveness*, many assumptions are made based on religious beliefs. As revealed previously through a message received from my father, many people believe that to heal completely the abused have to forgive the abuser. This is not true. Forgiveness is not a requirement or the first step in the healing process. While many religions may make it seem as though survivors must forgive those who have harmed them, this is a matter of spirituality that does not have to be shared by everyone. Forgiving the perpetuator does not have to be achieved to heal from childhood sexual abuse. However, the survivor must learn to forgive themselves and make peace with the child within who suffered the abuse. The survivor must know they did nothing wrong. Accepting this as fact requires consistent reminding and support that rape is always about the manipulation of power and control, and that men/boys can be sexually abused.

There is no writing exercise for this stage, but to help understand the connection between spirituality and forgiveness I have included a recount of my own struggles throughout this stage. As a male survivor of child sexual abuse journeying through the healing process, feel free to write about your experiences in your journal.

Not Damned to Hell

After my sexual abuse, I had many questions about my soul, virginity, heaven, hell, and the meaning of life. It was evident in the writings of my journals as a kid (which I still have) and my published short stores as an adult, that heaven, hell, and the fate of my soul was/is often on my mind. I questioned whether I would be permitted to enter heaven, if a person's virginity was a sign of their purity. My belief was that since my virginity was taken at such a young age, and by my sister, that I was damned to hell. Period. End of story. Do not pass go. It may seem ridiculous to others, but I believed that if I truly did not want to have sex, I would not have had an erection or begin to anticipate the occurrences over the course of the two years I was raped. It's for this reason I stopped taking communion in church. I believed I was not worthy of God's love, so I should not qualify to have my sins forgiven.

After two years of therapy, and consistently addressing the issue with my therapist I had reached a stalemate between my head and my heart. While my wife and two daughters went up to receive their blessing from the priest, I stayed in my seat and prayed for the protection and safety of my friends and family. Others throughout the church wondered why I never went to receive a blessing from the priest, even if I did not receive communion as a confirmed Catholic. Most of the congregation had become resigned to seeing the image of me sitting somberly in silent prayer as they passed, returning to their seats.

However, one Sunday morning something changed. I woke up and knew I needed to go to church. We went as a family and sat in the same seats we had always sat, but something still felt different. Deep down there was a feeling of something growing and rising to the surface. As the priest spoke the homily and explained how no one, even himself, deserved the compassion of God, but it was still given to everyone, it was one of the few instances in church when I felt he was truly talking to me. He explained that no matter a person's sins, they would always be forgiven if they asked. Tears came to my eyes as he finished, and I knew I was going to take communion, which I did.

At the end of the service that Sunday, I asked to address the congregation. As I stood in front of the church, I told them about my sexual abuse when I was eight years old and why I sat silently and prayed while others received their blessings. Tears streamed down my face as I explained how I thought I was damned to hell but had asked God for forgiveness on that day. When I finished, as the congregation clapped and cheered and I embraced Sarah, I felt renewed and more confident than ever before. I truly felt that the sexual abuse was not my fault, that God did not hate me.

The following Wednesday when I went to therapy, Susan praised my courage. She was very giddy and pleased as she explained that spirituality was a milestone I had to conquer on my own, and I had done it.

Does this mean that I go to church every Sunday and joined the choir? Not at all. Being a teacher, with a wife who is also a teacher, and attempting to raise two toddler girls without the help of family nearby to call on, means that getting out the door on Sunday by 9:20 is almost impossible. Does it mean I now take communion every Sunday? No. I still struggle with my relationship with God, but I still carry that feeling of love and pride with me from that day. It is something no one could have given, but a knowledge and spiritual connection that is all my own.

About a month later, I received a letter in the mail from the previous priest of our church, explaining how he had heard of my testimony and wanted to say a few words. His kind words and encouragement meant a lot and truly touched my heart. The letter is attached below.

SAINT FRANCIS
UNIVERSITY
FOUNDED 1847

July 22, 2016

Dear Kenny,

After I read in St Ann's bulletin about the book you wrote I checked it out. Needless to say I was surprised and upset to learn about the trouble and pain you were carrying. You always came across to me as a positive and cheerful person, and that just goes to show that we never know the burdens another is carrying. Despite the pain you describe there is great strength of character in your story. I often marvel at how differently people deal with adversity. Why are some overwhelmed and crushed, while others are able to rebound and move forward? I believe it is a combination of God's grace and your own inner strength.

I live near Johnstown, PA where there has been a long history of devastating floods. After the flood of 1977 I remember the scene of total chaos in the heart of the city. The town square was a sea of mud and debris and in the middle of it bloomed a bright yellow daffodil, a kind of defiance of the wreckage all around it. That's how I see you, and I hope you can see yourself, standing tall, rising above the mess, looking up at the sun and the sky, and connected to all the wonderful people in your life.

I'm glad you have found the courage to tell your story – even more to own it (and you are a gifted writer besides). You are a wonderful human being and a sign of hope in the face of so much that is bruised and broken in our world. Your personal witness can be a source of healing for others who suffer from many forms of injustice. And you're a gift to those 7th graders.

Please give my love to Sarah and your beautiful daughters as well, and know of my love and respect.

Praying for your peace,

Fr. Peter

Department of Philosophy and Religious Studies
P.O. Box 600, Loretto, PA 15940-0600   Phone: (814) 472-3372
www.francis.edu   471-1320

Chapter Nineteen
Resolution and Moving On

What makes Superman a hero is not that he has power, but that he has the wisdom and maturity to use the power wisely.

—Christopher Reeves

With Great Power ...

At the end of the journey toward healing from childhood sexual abuse, it is said that survivors will be able to resolve their past and move on. While this is true, the sexual abuse endured by survivors will remain a part of who they are. It will shape their actions, reactions, and views. While the abuse was a tragedy no child should have to endure, it allows survivors the ability to provide a perspective to a situation and way of life others who have not experienced sexual trauma and healed from it cannot have. Being a male survivor of child sexual abuse means you are stronger because you survived.

When this final stage of the healing process is reached, it almost becomes a responsibility to help others who are not in a good place and in need of healing from their own sexual abuse. It may take time and courage, but tell your story publicly if you can and change the societal belief of what it means to be a real man. Inform the public that men do and should express their emotions and intimacy. Become the guide of other young men and sons who no longer believe in the oversexualized stoic male. Prevent childhood sexual abuse by informing the public of its dangers and that men/boys can and do become sexually abused. This has been my goal in researching and writing this book. It tells my story and journey. Now, tell your story. Change lives as you mend your own to become the person you were meant to become—a real man.

"If—"

By Rudyard Kipling (1943)

If you can keep your head when all about you
Are losing theirs and blaming it on you,
If you can trust yourself when all men doubt you,
But make allowance for their doubting too;
If you can wait and not be tired by waiting,
Or being lied about, don't deal in lies,
Or being hated, don't give way to hating,
And yet don't look too good, not talk too wise:

If you can dream and not make dreams your master;
If you can think – and not make thoughts your aim;
If you can meet with Triumph and Disaster
And treat those two imposters just the same;
If you can bear to hear the truth you've spoke
Twisted by knaves to make a trap for fools,
Or watch the things you give life to, broken,
And stoop and build 'em up with worn-out tools:

If you can make one heap of all your winnings
And risk it on one turn of pitch-and-toss,
And lose, and start again at your beginnings
And never breathe a word about your loss;
If you can force your heart and nerve and sinew
To serve your turn long after they are gone,
And so hold on when there is nothing in you
Except the will which says to them: 'Hold on!'

If you can talk with crowds and keep your virtue,
Or walk with Kings – not lose common touch,
If neither foes not loving friends can hurt you,
If all men count with you, but none too much;
If you can fill the unforgiving minute
With sixty seconds' worth of distance run,
Yours is the Earth and everything that's in it,
And – which is more – you'll be a Man, my son!

Chapter Twenty
Writing Exercises

Directions:

This section contains all the writing exercises in the "Healing" portion of the guide, for quick easy access. Use your journal to complete the writing exercises as you move throughout the healing process. These exercises are not supposed to be completed quickly. They are meant to be thoughtful and allow time to reflect on your past sexual abuse. If you are not ready to complete an exercise, go to one you are ready to complete. If an exercise is too difficult to complete, put it away and return when you are ready. If you are in therapy or counseling for your childhood sexual abuse, take the journal with you to each session to take notes and help remember what should be practiced as you live from day to day and move through the healing process.

Writing Exercise #1: Remembering

Remembering the nature of your sexual abuse is difficult, no matter who the survivor may be. However, knowing you were sexually abused and remembering you were sexually abused is difficult. Pieces of the abuse may come out at separate times, and rather than memories you may experience physical sensations. Piecing these memories together will help you understand and accept that men and boys can be the victim of childhood sexual abuse. Writing the memories in a journal throughout the emergency stage will help in your healing to verify your emotions and that this did happen to you.

Writing Exercise #2: Knowing You're Not Superman

As mentioned in the previous section on heroes, as a male survivor you may have felt the need to hold the world on your shoulders and be Superman. However, throughout the emergency stage you may come to realize just how vulnerable you may be. This may mean over extending yourself and falling short of reaching your goal when you take on too many responsibilities. In the same way Superman was discussed as having low self-esteem when he is unable to accomplish everything, your self-esteem may be affected as your journey through the healing process, requiring needed self-care rather than prolonged mental abuse for viewing yourself as inadequate and not capable of accomplishing everything.

To complete this writing exercise, think about your past and remember a time you attempted to do more than you were capable of accomplishing. Write about how it made you feel, your thoughts at the time, and what happened afterward. This event can be during the emergency stage of your healing process or at an earlier time.

Writing Exercise #3: Your Hero Code

Everyone has a code that they live by, even if the code is never stated or written. This code guides the actions and beliefs of individuals. For some it may change slightly over time, but without understanding the code and how to change it, at its core it will remain the same.

In the section on heroes and the hero code, this was discussed in reference to the Flash. As a male survivor of child sexual abuse your code may be similar to Barry's and consist of absolute thoughts and black-and-white thinking. Although this view of the world may have allowed you to survive the trauma of your sexual abuse as a child, as an adult it can lead to the eventual transformation from becoming the hero of your own story to becoming the villain of others. As a child, it may have provided a source of strength, but over time the coping strategies may lose their needed effects.

Take the opportunity in your journal to explore your own hero code as you make the decision to heal. Explore the views of yourself, the world, and others with your therapist or counselor. It will allow both of you to see evidence of some form of the absolute thinking you have developed.

Over time, as you move through the healing process, your code will change and the absolute thoughts you held at the beginning of the process should change, as your brain begins to heal from the trauma of being sexually abused. When you feel you have made strides in your journey toward healing, rewrite your code. Take notice of the differences, discuss them with your therapist or counselor, and praise your achievements. No matter what, every survivor deserves to heal. Even you.

Writing Exercise #4: Revealing Your Secret Identity

Depending on where you are on your journey through the healing process, you may or may not have the ability to complete this writing exercise.

Every superhero has a secret identity that they feel must be kept in order to protect not only themselves, but also those closest to them. This appeal to secrecy as a form of strength is shared by many survivors as children, and may be why they were drawn to heroes in the first place. Unfortunately, the real world is not a comic book, and secrets only give strength to perpetrators and abusers. True strength comes from taking back control in the form of disclosing childhood sexual abuse and shedding light on past trauma. This creates knowledge, awareness, support, and trust where it was believed it did not exist.

If you have decided to regain this control and become strong enough to disclose the nature of your childhood sexual abuse, reflect on the experience. How did you react? How did you feel? If you have not told anyone about the nature of your sexual abuse as a child, it may be beneficial to write what you would say, and to whom you would tell. Predict what you believe their reaction may be. Reflect on how you felt while writing to prepare for being fully intimate and ridding yourself of the facades you believe are the only ways to survive.

Writing Exercise #5: Changing Your Thoughts

To help you understand the cognitive distortions you incur daily as a survivor, there is an exercise that can help lead you toward changing your thoughts in a positive way. It is called a cost-benefit analysis.

To complete this activity, it is recommended that you talk through the results with your counselor or therapist to ensure the correct conclusions are reached. First, write the thought you believe needs to be corrected, and then coincide with one or more of the listed cognitive distortions. For example, "What I did wasn't perfect, therefore I am worthless."

Next, read through the list of cognitive distortions that match the distorted thoughts. Some cognitive distortions that match the thought above are: all-or-nothing, overgeneralizations, mental filters, discounting the positives, minimization, emotional reasoning, labeling, personalization, and blame. Take the time to analyze why each distortion matches your thoughts.

Finally, change the thought to rid it of the cognitive distortions. This is the most difficult and requires the most practice. Changing the thought above to rid it of the cognitive distortions would be "I did my best." It is simple, but truthful and to the point.

Take the time and remain patient as you change the way you think. Over time, the process will become easier and the way you view yourself and your actions will change.

Cognitive Distortion Exercise: Changing Your Thoughts		
Distorted Thought	Cognitive Distortions	New Thought
What I did wasn't perfect, therefore I	all-or-nothing, overgeneralizations, mental filters, discounting the	I did my best and that's good enough.

am worthless.	positives, minimization, emotional reasoning, labeling, personalization, and blame	

Writing Exercise #6: Child, Parent, Adult Thinking

Although identifying the cognitive distortions in your thoughts is beneficial it is difficult and time consuming. A simple strategy to help change distorted automatic thoughts can be to label and change them from the thoughts of a child or parent to that of an adult.

- **Childish Thoughts:** These thoughts are filled with excuses and passing of blame to others. For example, "I didn't do anything wrong because it wasn't my responsibility," or "Bad things are always happening to me and not to anyone else." Rather than explore your role in the possible problem, your actions are justified and looked down on by others, when you believe they should be praised.

- **Parental Thoughts:** These thoughts are filled with "should" and "must" statements, making the survivor believe they have no choice. Examples are: "I didn't do anything to deserve attention," or "I have to follow the rules."

- **Adult Thoughts:** The goal of this exercise is to reframe the automatic thoughts so that they are longer those of an uncompromising parent or a child controlled by their needs and wants. For example, "I *do* the best I can." Changing these automatic thoughts to resemble those of an adult takes practice and help.

In this writing exercise, work with you therapist, counselor, or support system to identify your automatic thoughts that are those of a child or parent, and how to reframe them to those of an adult. To help with this process use the graphic organizer below.

Automatic Thought Exercise				
Automatic Thought	**Childish Reasoning**	**Parental Reasoning**	**Cognitive Distortions**	**Adult Thought**
Bad things are always happening to me and no one else.	X		overgeneralizations, mental filters, discounting the positives, labeling	I do the best I can.

Writing Exercise #7: A Letter to the Past

Write a letter to the little boy who was abused as a child. Tell him the good things he has to offer the world. Provide encouragement that the future will get better. Say the things you wish would have been said by your parents or family when you were young and life seemed impossible to bear.

Writing Exercise #8: What If . . .

Following your sexual abuse, you may have developed questions as an adult about who you could have been or what you could have done. These questions will cause you to mourn the life and experiences you lost and that were taken. For this writing exercise, write those questions you may have exploring the possibility of the life you would have had without being sexually abused. After writing these questions, list and explain the things you have to mourn the loss of. This list can and should be added to as you move throughout the healing process.

This is not a race. Write, rest, then return to reflect and add.

References

Comics, Books, Poems, and Articles Referenced Throughout the Text

Action Comics #1: "Superman, Champion of the Oppressed" (1938)

Action Comics #242: "The Super-Duel in Space" (1958)

Action Comics #544: "Luthor Unleashed" (1983)

Adventure Comics #260: "How Aquaman Got His Powers" (1959)

Adventure Comics #269: "The Kid from Atlantis" (1960)

Adventure Comics #452: "Dark Destiny, Deadly Dreams" (1977)

Aquaman #2: "Single Wet Female" (1994)

Batman #1: "The Legend of the Batman – Who He Is and How He Came to Be" (1940)

Batman #408: "Did Robin Die Tonight?" (1987)

Batman #427: "Death in the Family" Part 2 (1988)

Batman #442: "A Lonely Place of Dying," Part 5 (1989)

Batman #497: "Broken Bat" (1993)

Batman #657: "Batman and Son," Part 3 (2006)

Batman Annual #14: "The Eye of the Beholder" (1990)

Batman: Legends of the Dark Knight #66: "Going Sane," Part Two (1994)

Batman Special #1: ". . . The Player on the Other Side" (1984)

Crisis on Infinite Earths #8: "A Flash of the Lightning!" (1985)

Detective Comics #38: "Robin, The Boy Wonder" (1940)

Detective Comics #574: ". . . My Beginning . . . And My Probable End" (1987)

Detective Comics #633: "Identity Crisis" (1991)

Flash Comics #1: "Origins of the Flash" (1940)

Flashpoint (2011)

Green Lantern / Green Arrow #85-86: "Snowbirds Don't Fly" and "They Say It'll Kill Me … But They Won't Say When" (1971)

"If—" by Rudyard Kipling (1943)

Justice League of America Annual #2: "The End of the Justice League" (1984)

L.E.G.I.O.N. '91 #31: "Where Dreams End" (1991)

Nightwing #101: "Nightwing: Year One," Part 1 (2005)

Raped Black Male: A Memoir by Kenneth Rogers Jr. (2016)

Relationship of Childhood Abuse and Household Dysfunction to Many of the Leading Causes of Death in Adults: The Adverse Childhood Experiences (ACE) Study (1998)

Real Boys: Rescuing Our Sons from the Myths of Boyhood. By William S. Pollack (1999)

Secret Origins Annual #2: "The Unforgiving Minute" (1998)

Showcase #4: "The Mystery of the Human Thunderbolt!" (1956)

Substance Abuse and Mental Health Services Administration (2009)

Superman #53: "The Origin of Superman" (1948)

Superman #129: "The Girl in Superman's Past" (1959)

Superman #164: "The Showdown Between Luthor and Superman" (1963)

Superman #276: "Make Way for Captain Thunder" (1974)

The Batman Chronicles #3: "The First Cut Is the Deepest" (1996)

The Courage to Heal: A Guide for Women Survivors of Child Sexual Abuse. By Ellen Bass and Laura Davis (2008)

The Hero With A Thousand Faces. By Joseph Campbell (1949)

The Power of SHAZAM #1: "Things Change" (1995)

Thoughts in Italics: "Action Guy" By Kenneth Rogers Jr. (2007)

Whiz Comics #2: "Introducing Captain Marvel" (1940)

Hero and Villain Glossary

A

Alfred Pennyworth: The butler and surrogate father of Bruce Wayne.

Aquababy/Arthur Jr.: The son of Aquaman and Mera who was killed by the villain Black Manta.

Aqualad/Garth: The sidekick of Aquaman. Originally a citizen of Atlantis, he was exiled from the city because of his fear of fish. After curing Aqualad of his fear, Aquaman took in the boy as his sidekick.

Aquaman: The superhero able to breathe underwater and communicate with sea life. Actually named Arthur Curry, Aquaman was born with his abilities when his mother was outcast from the lost city of Atlantis and married a human.

Arthur Curry: The name of Aquaman that was given to him by his human father and Atlantian mother.

B

Bane: Villain in Batman's Rogue Gallery who discovers Batman's secret identity and breaks his back. Bane has super strength that he receives from injections known as Venom.

Barry Allen: The second person to call themselves the Flash. Unlike Jay Garrick, the first Flash, Barry's character exists on an Earth in an alternate dimension known as Earth 2. Also unlike Jay, Barry received his powers after lightning struck him, dowsing him with chemicals and giving him the ability of super speed.

Batman: The superhero and mortal also known as "The Dark Knight" and "The World's Greatest Detective." His secret identity is billionaire playboy Bruce Wayne. After the death of his parents, Bruce Wayne left Gotham and began training for his war on crime as Batman. Throughout Japan, China, Nepal, Africa, and the Middle East, he trained in all forms of hand-to-hand combat. To better his mind, he studied at the Berlin School of Science and Cambridge University. He mastered the languages of Arabic, Chinese, Japanese, Tibetan, Eskimo, Latin, French, German, Spanish, and Kryptonese. By his early twenties, he returned to Gotham and used the skills he learned to become Batman.

Billy Batson: The secret identity of Captain Marvel. He was given the ability to transform into Captain Marvel by the ancient wizard, Shazam. To become the world's mightiest mortal, all Billy must do is yell the name of the wizard and the transformation is complete with the striking of a lightning bolt. He is able to transform back into Billy Batson by yelling "Shazam" a second time.

Brainiac: An alien who shrank Earth cities and its inhabitants to repopulate his planet.

Bruce Wayne: Billionaire playboy who owns and operates Wayne Enterprises. As a boy, Bruce lost his parents, Thomas and Martha Wayne, when they were murdered by Joe Chill. After their murder, Bruce vowed to avenge their death by fighting crime in Gotham City. After years of training across the world, he returned to Gotham and became Batman.

C

Captain Marvel: Also known as "The World's Mightest Mortal," he has magical powers that allow him to fly and have super strength. Although he has the appearance of a man, he is actually a little boy known as Billy Batson. He was given his powers by the wizard, Shazam, which is an acronym for the abilities he possesses from the Greek gods and heroes: Solomon's wisdom, **H**ercules's strength, **A**tlas's stamina, **Z**eus's power, **A**chilles' courage, and **M**ercury's speed.

Captain Thunder: The hero/villain in *Superman #276* who was meant to represent Captain Marvel. Like Captain Marvel, Captain Thunder's secret identity is a little boy, Willie Fawcett. Unlike

Captain Marvel, his powers do not come from an ancient wizard endowed with powers from Greek heroes and gods. Instead, Captain Thunder's powers came from a Native American shaman who endowed him powers from the Native American culture: a **T**ornado's power, a **H**are's speed, **U**ncas's bravery, **N**ature's wisdom, **D**iamond's toughness, **E**agle's flight, and **R**am's tenacity.

Clark Kent: Often described as mild-mannered, Clark Kent is a reporter for the newspaper the *Daily Planet* in Metropolis. While wearing glasses and portraying himself as weak and not assertive, he is the secret identity of Superman. He was raised by Jonathan and Martha Kent in Smallville, Kansas, after being found in a spaceship from his home planet Krypton. His Kryptonian name is Kal-El, and his Kryptonian birth parents are Jor-El and Lar-El.

D

Damian Wayne: The son of Bruce Wayne and Talia al Ghul, and the current Robin. He was raised by his mother until the age of seven as an assassin and a member of the League of Shadows. When Bruce discovered that Damian was his son, he took the boy in. Unlike the other Robins, except perhaps Jason Todd, Damian had no problem killing. After years of mentoring, eventually Damian learned not to kill and become the new Robin.

Dick Grayson: The first person to wear the costume and become Robin, Batman's sidekick. As a child, he was a member of the traveling circus act known as "The Flying Graysons," with his mother and father. After the murder of his parents, Bruce Wayne adopted the boy and trained him to use acrobatic skills to fight crime as Batman's sidekick, Robin. Over time, Dick yearned to move from Batman's shadow as Robin and became the hero Nightwing.

F

Flash: The superhero who has the ability of super speed. Originally the hero acquired his powers after inhaling the vapors of hard water. Later, the hero's powers originated from a strike of lightning and a mixture of chemicals, allowing him to tap into and use the "Speedforce." The three heroes who have worn the costume and called themselves the Flash are Jay Garrick, Barry Allen, and Wally West.

G

Green Arrow: The hero who fights crime using a bow and arrow. Dressed in green and resembling Robin Hood, Oliver Queen uses his superb marksmanship to battle social injustices as well as crime.

Green Lantern: The superhero who fights crime with the power of a ring that has the ability to materialize anything the hero visualizes into solid objects that are green. The owners of the rings are chosen by aliens known as the Guardians and then initiated as members of the Green Lantern Corps. There have been a number of Green Lanterns from Earth. The most notable ones are Hal Jordan, John Stewart, and Kyle Reiner.

H

Harvey Dent: Gotham City district attorney who became the villain Two-Face after having acid thrown onto one half of his face.

J

James Gordon: Gotham City police commissioner.

Jason Todd: The second person to wear the Robin costume. After stealing the wheels off the Batmobile on the anniversary of the death of Bruce Wayne's parents, he adopted the boy and trained him to be the new Robin. Unfortunately, he was beaten and murdered by the Joker after finding his mother in Africa, opening the position for Robin number three to be filled by Tim Drake.

Jay Garrick: The original secret identity of the Flash when he was first created in the 1940s. As a scientist, Jay inhaled the chemical fumes of hard water and found he had the ability to run at super speed. After college, he decided to use his powers to become the Flash and based his costume's design after the Greek god Mercury.

Joker: The archnemesis of Batman who thrives on chaos. Dressed as a clown with a white face, green hair, and a wide grin, he often leaves his villains dead, their face carved with a smile or laughing.

Joe Chill: The murderer of Thomas and Martha Wayne.

Jonathan Kent: Adopted father of Clark Kent

Jor-El: The birth father of Kal-El. To save his son from the dying planet Krypton, he built a spaceship and sent his son to Earth, were he would be found and renamed Clark Kent and become the superhero Superman.

Joseph Kerr: The alternate personality developed by the Joker in an attempt to become sane.

K

Kal-El: The Kryptonian name/identity of Superman/Clark Kent, given to him by his Kryptonian parents, Jor-El and Lar-El.

L

Lar-El: The birth mother of Kal-El. To save her son, she and her husband, Jor-El, sent their son to Earth to escape their dying planet, Krypton. Later, Kal-El would be renamed Clark Kent and become Superman.

Leslie Thompkins: A surgeon and the adopted mother of Bruce Wayne.

Lex Luthor: The archnemesis of Superman who wants nothing more than to see the superhero suffer and die. He is extremely intelligent, but devotes all of his resources toward destroying the Man of Steel.

Lori Lemaris: The love interest of Clark Kent/Superman who was a mermaid from Atlantis.

Lois Lane: Reporter for the *Daily Planet* and love interest of Superman.

M

Martha Kent: Adopted mother of Clark Kent

Martha Wayne: The mother of Bruce Wayne who was murdered in Park Row at 10:27 on the night of June 26 after attending the movie *The Mask of Zorro* with her family. Her son, Bruce, would be the only survivor and would eventually become the hero Batman.

Mera: The wife of Aquaman.

N

Nightwing: The first Robin, Dick Grayson, who quit being the Boy Wonder and became his own hero.

O

Oliver Queen: The secret identity of the Green Arrow.

R

Robin: Also known as "The Boy Wonder," he is Batman's sidekick. Dressed in red, green, and yellow, he was meant to represent Robin Hood in name and appearance. Over the years of Batman's existence, there have been many people (and a robot) who have put on the Robin costume to fight beside the Dark Knight. The most notable Robins are Dick Grayson, Jason Todd, Tim Drake, and Damian Wayne.

Roy "Speedy" Harper: The sidekick of the Green Arrow who becomes addicted to drugs but later becomes sober. Like the hero, he fights crime using a bow and arrow.

S

Shazam: The ancient wizard who gave Billy Batson the ability to transform into Captain Marvel.

Superman: Known by man as "The Man of Steel," Superman is a superhero who has the ability to fly, run at super speed, have super strength, and x-ray vision. The *S* symbol on his chest is a sign of hope for many characters throughout the DC universe and the real world. His secret identity is Clark Kent, a news reporter for the *Daily Planet*. Although raised by human parents John and Martha Kent in Smallville, Kansas, he is actually an alien from the planet Krypton. His Kryptonian name is Kal-El, and his Kryptonian birth parents are Jor-El and Lar-El.

Synaptic Kid: A villain who has the ability to read minds and went crazy after reading the mind of Batman in an attempt to reveal his secret identity.

T

Talia al Ghul: Mother of Damian Wayne, lover of Bruce Wayne, daughter of Ra's al Ghul, and member of the League of Shadows.

Thomas Wayne: The father of Bruce Wayne who was murdered in Park Row at 10:27 on the night of June 26 by Joe Chill from a gunshot. He was with his wife, Martha, who also died, and his son, Bruce, who lived and would later become Batman.

Tim Drake: The third person to wear the Robin costume. After discovering the secret identities of Robin number one, Dick Grayson, and Batman as Bruce Wayne, he convinced the heroes to allow him to become the new Robin. Afraid of losing another Robin after the murder of Jason Todd at the hands of the Joker, Batman refused. However, after saving Batman and Nightwing from Two-Face, Batman agreed. Unlike the previous two Robins, Tim was not adopted by Bruce Wayne. Instead, he had his own family he reported back to each morning after fighting crime.

Two-Face: Villain of Batman's Rogue Gallery who decides the fate of his victims with the flip of a two-headed silver dollar that is scarred on one side. Formerly Gotham City district attorney Harvey Dent, he became a villain after having acid thrown onto one half of his face, scarring one side and leaving the other untouched.

V

Victor Zsasz/Mister Zsas: Villain in Batman's Rogue Gallery who kills his victims and leaves their bodies in lifelike poses. After killing his victims, he cuts a mark into his own skin to tally his victims and remind himself that even he is human.

W

Wally West: The superhero who was struck by lightning and dowsed with chemicals as a boy, giving him the ability of super speed. Originally, he was Kid Flash, the sidekick of Barry Allen's Flash. However, after Barry's death, Wally took on the mantle of becoming the new Flash.

Willie Fawcett: The boy in *Superman #276* who was meant to represent Billy Batson. In the same way Billy could transform into Captain Marvel after yelling the name Shazam, Willie could transform into Captain Thunder after yelling "Thunder" and rubbing his belt buckle. Instead of being given the powers by an ancient wizard, Willie was given his power by an old Native American shaman.

CPSIA information can be obtained
at www.ICGtesting.com
Printed in the USA
LVOW03s1733140917
548554LV00001B/5/P